MW00882041

LIFE
in the
ELECTRIC CHAIR

LIFE
in the
ELECTRIC CHAIR

A MAN AND HIS WIFE EXPLORE A LIFE ON WHEELS

DAN WEST

authorHOUSE®

AuthorHouse™
1663 Liberty Drive
Bloomington, IN 47403
www.authorhouse.com
Phone: 1-800-839-8640

© *2012 by Dan West. All rights reserved.*

No part of this book may be reproduced, stored in a retrieval system, or transmitted by any means without the written permission of the author.

Published by AuthorHouse   04/03/2012

ISBN: 978-1-4685-7347-3 (sc)
ISBN: 978-1-4685-7346-6 (hc)
ISBN: 978-1-4685-7345-9 (e)

Library of Congress Control Number: 2012905494

Any people depicted in stock imagery provided by Thinkstock are models, and such images are being used for illustrative purposes only.
Certain stock imagery © Thinkstock.

This book is printed on acid-free paper.

Because of the dynamic nature of the Internet, any web addresses or links contained in this book may have changed since publication and may no longer be valid. The views expressed in this work are solely those of the author and do not necessarily reflect the views of the publisher, and the publisher hereby disclaims any responsibility for them.

Table of Contents

Acknowledgements

My wife must be thanked for all her great encouragement, and help proofing the whole story. She also helped quite a bit on the glossary. She knew many of the medical words, and helped in researching what they all meant. I do not know what I would have done without all of her help. A friend of hers also helped proof the whole text.

I also had major help from the Dragon-Speaking Naturally software by Nuance. Since I cannot write, and do not type very well, I used this speech recognition software. It takes what I say and translates it into written form. It is not perfect, but without it I could not have written this. I would go back and make corrections where needed, but the vast majority was handled by this software.

Overview

I have been described as an enigma by every doctor I have come across. No one seems to know what is going on, so I go from one doctor to the next. Since I love stories, this is a story about my life after I got this strange disease, with a few short stories about my life before, and how my wife and I cope. We all have stories about our lives, and I just want to share what has been going on in my life and how it affects my family and others.

I had been feeling a little weird and went to see the doctor and while we were waiting for test results, we went camping, and we noticed that things were different. Before, I was an active normal guy; I played softball, basketball, golf, snow skied, water skied and rode a motorcycle. Hey, I was pretty cool. These all require balance, and now I had very little. I went to church, and people were praying for me. I thought this problem would be over soon, so I did not think much about it at that time. The body of believers stepped up when things were a little shaky.

Doctors included some pretty impressive titles; Neurologists from Stanford, UCSF, Kaiser, NIH (National Institute of Health) in Maryland, Mayo clinic, UC Berkeley, and Cal Pacific Med center, with doctors specializing in specific diseases such as Lymphatiod Granulomatosis, Neurosarcadosis, Lyme disease, Acute Disseminated Encephalomyelitis, and Ataxia. Those are some big words, and it will be shared how they were ruled out, or confirmed by different doctors. There were all kinds of treatments given as an attempt to eradicate the suspected disease. I had the added confusion of disagreement among physicians of different reputable institutes, as to what actually was happening. It was very frustrating not knowing exactly what to do.

The first couple of years I was able to walk and even built a sub-standard shed in the back yard. My balance was still off and I could not drive. I could still write and handle bills, but my writing was degrading slowly. Now, I cannot write. Then I went to a walker for about a year, and now have been in this electric chair.

My wife, Marcia, is great. She does most of the things I cannot do. Of course, we do have some disagreements. She always wants me to go places and have people over. I don't always agree, and so we have to discuss what the plans are. Marcia is better at making sure all systems are go before making any plans. We communicate pretty well, but we do have some issues that we continually need to be aware of.

My family and my wife's family are normal, but like everyone, they all carry their own baggage. Each has a great story to tell. I'm only going to share about my immediate family, and my wife's. Otherwise, it would get really crazy trying to talk about all of our relatives. Most are physically close. I have only one brother in Oregon and Marcia has two brothers, one in San Diego and one here, and one sister about 15 miles from here.

Most friends of ours are still around and continue to be friends to this day. Some are close by, and that is great, but some are far away, only it does not take long to get back on track. The church has been great, too.

There are plenty of frustrations. It is easy to get frustrated, as it seems like something inconvenient is happening all the time. What I have to do is just carry on, and trust that God is in control. Otherwise, it is easy to make unwise demands.

I was wondering about sex issues, but my son said he would rather have a sharp stick poked in his eye, so I decided to leave it out.

A few times I mention things done in the past, that would not be tolerated today. It almost implies that things were handled better then. For me, things worked out, but there were plenty of bad things happening, like racism and unequal rights for women. There many good rules/regulations, but there are many that make no sense to me.

There is one thing I want to mention. I want to try to briefly describe what my disease is like. For example, if everything is nerve related, imagine my deaf son has less nerves for hearing. Let's say he is normal, he just cannot hear. Now I come along, and have a whole lot less nerves, all over the place. There are many things I cannot do; I am not normal. People look at me and think I am fine, but I am not. They just do not look for the shakiness and the lack of fine motor skills. My slow voice says something. I cannot focus on things as well. My eyesight is fine, but I have fewer nerves, so it takes more time to focus on things properly. When I am in a vehicle, it takes me time to focus on things, but sometimes they are by me before I know it, and I miss out. My hearing is fine, but it helps if I hear things directly. I really have to concentrate if something is coming from another room. Many times I do not get it all. It is probably my pride that makes me come across as "normal," but I am not. In the Mel Brooks comedy, 'Young Frankenstein', the hunchback (Marty Fieldman), picks out what he thinks is the normal brain of A.B.Normal. It is not. I want to be treated as normal, just be aware that I am a little abeeenormal. Most of us want to look "normal," but things happen that others are not aware of. I sometimes feel like I am a 60 year old in a 100 year old body.

So, What Happened?

First, some background/history. I was born in Oakland, California, but lived in San Lorenzo, a few miles away, in August of 1951. We moved to another house in January 1955, in Centerville (later Fremont, California). TVs were now available, and we actually got one. They were only available in black and white, and had no remote control—imagine that. My dad got to know a minister and soon we were going to church. Many years later, I was moderator of the senior high youth group. My parents were strict, but I was rather mischievous. I started kindergarten in September of that year and was continually hassled by a first grade girl. One day, I dragged the girl into the empty boy's bathroom. I was about to run out, but I saw her lying there face down, and I pulled down her underpants, then ran back to my class. She must have been too embarrassed to tell anyone, and I never got hassled again. Today, if she told, I would probably have been sent to juvenile hall as a sexual deviant.

Unfortunately, being mischievous also had its downside. In first grade, it was raining and the teacher said to stay out of it. Of course, I went out in it and then noticed her looking at me. I started running to where it was dry, but ran into a big steel girder. I had a big goose bump on my head. I got sick. My head has taken a beating over the years. In second grade, I fell off some playground equipment onto my head. I felt sick. In fifth grade, I slipped and hit my head in some sprinkler water that we were not supposed to play in. I felt sick. I also got in a fight in the fifth grade.

A six grade boy thought he was cool and said something to me that I did not like. We got into a fight and he was cleaning my clock when the principal arrived. The bell rang and kids went to their classes, but the principal allowed us to fight for a little longer. I think the principal liked the fact that I was getting beaten soundly. I ended up with two black eyes and an upper lip that looked like raw hamburger. My parents talked to the principal, but I still had to go to school the next day. All the kids stared and stared. I felt foolish, but I had no choice, I had to go. There would be no more fights until the 11th grade. I had learned a valuable lesson. Today, the principal would probably be fired and the school district would get sued.

In seventh grade I agreed to mow the lawn of my parents' friends' neighbor. I agreed with the husband to mow the front lawn for a month at a certain price. When I went to collect after a month, the wife answered the door and offered me a lower price. I explained that the husband and I had already agreed on a price. She said that he was not available and that she was in charge. My dad was waiting in the car, but I got angry and used the B word. My dad sensed something was wrong and got out of the car. The lady told him to get back in the car, take me and leave. So we did. The friends of my parents were able to make things right. I returned, apologized, and took the lower price. However, I went back for the next few years on Halloween and threw eggs at the house. I knew it was wrong, but it felt good. Feelings may tell you to do something, but it is not always right.

Speaking of Halloween, one year, when I was in junior high, I was walking a half mile to church when I decided to detour and go to the nearby shopping center, where a bunch of kids were celebrating Halloween. There were about 200 kids there, throwing water balloons, eggs, and pumpkins. The police cruised by, but the kids were good when they saw them. I found myself being chased by kids in a car with water balloons. I had an egg in each hand as I ran to get a way. I was running hard and did not see some ground cover. I tripped and went flying, and landed on grass. The eggs were still whole, so I got up and hid so they could not find me. I was lucky.

In eighth and 11th grade, I also played tackle football. I wrestled and played basketball in high school. On the last day of high school, when I was a senior, I was riding in the backseat of a VW with some friends, without wearing seatbelts. Suddenly, we were chased by a truck with a fire extinguisher, and guys were trying to spray us with water. We tried to get a way, but we had a slow car. We turned a corner to sharp and rolled the car over one time, landing upright. The window next to me had been knocked out and I had glass in my belly button. The driver was okay, but his elbow had broken the nose of the passenger in the front seat. The problem was that the car belonged to the passenger. So, the driver felt really bad. When the police showed up, we did not say that we were being chased, but I think the officer knew. We laughed afterwards, but we were really lucky. My head had been rattled around, but I felt fine.

I played basketball in Junior college, and dove for the ball a lot. I was also in a motorcycle accident in 1988 and bumped my head. I was going slowly in between lanes during commute hour when a truck pulled out in front of me. His bumper caught my engine guard and I went flying through the windshield of the motorcycle. We were not going very fast, but I did land on the pavement surrounded by cars. I was able to go to work, but by noon my whole body was sore. Fortunately, I was wearing a helmet.

I also played basketball with some friends at work. One day we were playing another team and I backed up and fell, and cracked my head on the cement. I stayed out for a while, but went back in and played very well. I had a friend follow me home, as I was not feeling 100%. Later that night I threw up and went to the doctor. He said I had a mild concussion and that I would be okay in a few days. I was snow skiing and water skiing, too, and had some great falls. Maybe all this hitting my head had its consequences, many years later. Only God knows.

During Spring break (April) 2001, a group of high-school kids decided cold weather beach camping in Half Moon Bay, California, would be a blast. I traveled as the senior leader with one of the area directors of our local Young Life group. Young Life is a Christian ministry to high school kids started by Jim

Rayburn back in the early 1940s. He was a minister in Texas who wanted unchurched kids to enjoy spiritual things, and have fun doing them. It is now an international organization, with clubs all over the world. At the campground, it was rainy and I laid in some weeds during a game, plus, a bout of "whip-lash" hit my neck while we were playing soft-ball in the sand later the next day. This left me a bit out of sorts in the days that followed. I felt tired and had a cold when I got home.

I was also playing right field on a city recreation softball team. The game had started at 9 o'clock at night and for an April day the weather was pretty nice. The batter hit a low line drive to right field. The ball bounced and I dove for it, as it was way to my left. I was able to stop the ball and throw it in, but hit the left side of my head and chipped my tooth. I felt fine. Finally, the opposing team had three outs and we were up. I was second at bat this particular inning. Since I was an older player, 49, I usually was 9th out of 10 in the batting order. My ups came and I actually got a hit and landed on first base. The leadoff hitter came up with two outs and hit the ball sharply up the middle and I took off. As I rounded second heading for third, I felt a little strange, but was safe sliding into third. The next guy hit a single up the middle and I scored easily. As I went back to the bench, the coach said I looked a little strange when I rounded second going to third, kind of like I was running at a 45 degree angle. The other players thought I had too much to drink and just laughed. I agreed with the coach, but told him I was fine. I finished the game and drove home (unfortunately, that was my last game, I just did not know it yet.)

The next day at work I noticed my writing was a little different. I felt okay, but my fine motor skills were not so fine. I remember thinking I could get a few days off because of this "weirdness." Little did I know this was the beginning of the end of my working days. I kept on at work for the next few weeks as things became progressively worse. We checked in with the doctor, hoping for an easy answer. She said it was probably Labrynthitis, (an inner ear infection) and would go away in a few days. I was slowly getting worse after a week, and went back to the hospital, with a different doctor. He finally asked if I was spinning in my head, then said, "No spinning, no Labrynthitis," and scheduled an MRI May 31st, to see if we could visualize a problem.

In the meantime, on Memorial Day weekend we went camping at Lake Shasta, in northern California, and I struggled to get pulled out of the water behind our boat on one ski. I had been skiing since the early 60s so I did not anticipate a problem. When I was much younger, my dad had been given a small ski-boat hull, and he and a neighbor built the insides and also built a trailer to pull it. I learned to double ski and single ski, and we went about once a month during the summer for a number of years. In my college years, I went camping with a friend and his family, and their ski boat. I only was able to ski a few times a year. After I was married, and had a couple of kids, we bought a used ski boat. We then started camping at a lake and also house boating for a week at Lake Shasta with friends. I was getting good and I could make it through the water ski course.

Now, I tried to get up several times and I usually got up on the first or second try. I could not get up. In my 30+ years of water skiing, I could not maintain my balance. My brother and oldest son had accompanied me, and were shocked. They knew I was not quite 100%, and I thought I saw some watery eyes. I could walk around, but did not have the coordination to ski. I was at a loss. My wife drove most of the way home, much to her dismay, as she never offered to drive the truck with a trailer in tow. I slept in the back of the covered truck, my wife and I preoccupied with the thought something had gone terribly wrong.

I Am Tired

T he information in this chapter is good, but I find it too medical for me. We got back home from Lake Shasta, and got the MRI. It showed there was inflammation in the brain noted by white markings on the film. They ran a few blood tests and attempted to get the inflammation under control. When they did a blood draw, I actually had veins. They would later vanish, since I had so many blood draws.

Doctor R, a neurologist, did blood tests and head-skull x-rays. Nystagmus, a loss of muscle control in the eyes, causing them to move involuntarily back and forth and Ataxia, a jerky gross motor movement, were prominent along with tingling in both of my hands. The MRI was a positive read, meaning something was amiss. In my particular case, the cerebella and pons region had white dots in random areas indicating inflammation. Doctor S, another neurologist, did a chest x-ray and ordered a Lumbar Puncture (L.P.) study. She also decided a chest x-ray was in order to see if inflammation was also in the lungs. She did the L.P. and found the results to be negative, meaning no disease in the spinal fluid. There was an increase in finger tingling and noticeable bilaterally. Marcia, my wife who is an R.N., notified Doctor K, a neurologist at the hospital where she works, as a "second opinion." He had never seen the likes of such markings on an MRI and decided immediate intervention was necessary. He notified the doctor by phone and recommended high doses of steroids to be given at once. The doctor, at a loss for a better solution, infused 1 Gram (1 quart for you non-medical types) of steroids intravenously in two hour infusions, guessing the diagnosis was: ADEM (acute disseminated encephalomyelitis).

On June 12th, the headache on both sides of the temporal areas stopped after steroid infusion. The blood pressure taken was normal at: 133/81. Headaches were reported prior to treatments and Doctor N, our number one neurologist, was notified. I was feeling 20% better. I was still tired.

June 15th Doctor N recommended us to see Doctor G at a nearby hospital. He is a renowned neurologist in Multiple Sclerosis and we wanted to rule this condition out, or we just wanted the truth and to be set free by knowing what we were up against.

We called a dear nursing friend, who gave a massage to my sore back. Surges, I like to call them, started, meaning episodes where I stuttered or had a seizure like spasm, yet not a seizure. I was still able to walk 1-1/4 mile around our local Newark Lake, but needed hand holding due to my shaky gait.

Physical Therapist, Sue V, evaluated my movements on June 21st. She noted my left side was stronger than my right. She thought spinal compressions could be the culprit. We made an E.R. visit and saw Doctor M to consult him on the surges but he was afraid to recommend anything without us consulting a neurologist. Doctor R recommended increasing Prednisone to 70 mg/day. Doctor K was notified of my surges of slurred speech and recommended an EEG, which was never ordered. I continued "surges" 10-20 times an hour but saw improvement with my gait and my strabismus. We attributed this to the anti-inflammatory properties of the steroids.

Doctor N was notified about surges and a CAT scan was ordered. We met Doctor A, yet another neurologist, who recommended trying Tegretol. Knowing Tegretol was used for seizures, it frightened us in the prospect of this being what was going on neurologically. He assured us that sometimes the slurred speech is improved with this medication in patients that have Multiple Sclerosis or speech issues.

In fear of the unknown, we once again consulted with Doctor K, who agreed with the Tegretol. The June 28th MRI #2 showed a marked improvement. The surges and slurred speech decreased with Tegretol.

Doctor G did a physical exam and recommended weaning off Prednisone, but to continue with the Tegretol. ANA (anti-nuclear-antibodies) were drawn to check for Lupus, which thankfully was negative, or ruled out. On the last day of Prednisone and Tegretol, we attended a wedding. My face was puffy from the steroids but since I had been using the weaning process of getting off of the steroids I found myself to be rather comfortable and even able to ambulate slowly but more sure footed. I was still tired.

From July 24th to Aug.4th, we had planned a Hawaii vacation. Never in our wildest dreams did we think this inflammatory issue was going to take this long to resolve.

We thought this to be a virus, or a onetime acute attack of the brain. We confirmed improvement by Doctor N prior to going and happily gathered up our boys to spend my Hawaii 5-0 in Maui. I was to turn 50 on August 1. We returned from Hawaii with concerns. Near the end of our 10 day stay I was unable to drive, not trusting my muscle abilities, and I also noted an increase in "wobbliness." Doctor R was given the message about wobbliness.

On Aug. 20th, we were scheduled for MRI #3, which, much to our dismay, was worse than the first time!! The same cerebella site had white areas all around with some in the pons and medulla. Since steroids had helped before, we had to start 1 gram of steroid infusions for 5 days. Another L.P. by Doctor N was ordered to look for bands cells that come from our white blood cells. No cells in the L.P. were found, a good sign, and Prednisone was started orally at 60mg a day.

I started feeling surges again, but this time not with the speech. There was no recommendation for Tegretol. My right arm was numb in the morning. The tips of my fingers were a tiny bit numb. The frequency of surges was irregular and I'm a regular guy, trying to make sense out of my irregular patterns. I had a light headed rush and urgency to pee. Doctor N recommended Tegretol again. Prednisone is the only anti-inflammatory drug that goes to work in a crisis. Prilosec was given to me to relieve my stomach from any issues with ulcers, a side effect of steroids, or Prednisone. Tegretol worked as an "anti-surg" med for me. September 20th, four days after my wife's birthday, was celebrated quietly. We had a visit with Doctor G at a major university, who decided we did not have Multiple Sclerosis, but perhaps a Rheumatology issue like Neurosarcodosis. Doctor S, a renowned Rheumatologist, decided we needed to see him in October. I was still tired.

Ah yes, the infamous L.P. was recommended again to make sure I did not inherit yet another problem. Doctor N found the cerebral fluid to be within normal limits. Doctor S and Doctor R evaluated me and recommended a Cerebral Angiogram to rule out Neurosarcodosis. Blood was drawn once again. A complete blood count, a clotting time, and my electrolytes and all were in normal limits. On Halloween, I was on my last dose of oral Prednisone, thankfully. Due to the buzz and euphoria, I was feeling out of it most of the time. November was upon us and Doctor H gave us a report on the angiogram, stating our arteries were as clear as a bell, another rule out maneuver, yet not confirmed diagnosis. Should we be glad or sad? We were neutral.

Doctor N decided to at least work on the immune system with some liquid gold, called Gamma Globulin, 35 grams for five days. Each bottle runs $1000, so we felt special. Perhaps boosting the immune system concept would stop this maddening inflammatory process. We started this on November 9th. On Nov. 13th, just four days after the infusions, I felt extremely ataxic and had an amazing buzz, and no noted change with the infusion. We took another MRI of the brain, #4, and Doctor M, a neuro-surgeon, viewed the find.

In the meantime, we got alternative treatments with a chiropractor in San Jose. This Doctor C is one of a few that know a procedure called the Axil Manipulation. This procedure can be done with 110 volts to the neck and it re-aligns the two axils that are "floating" in the cervical column, the only two bones without discs. This all sounded plausible to us, so we allowed the volts to hit "pop" like a jack hammer. That would be a pay out of your pocket and take your own risk kind of visit.

None the worse for wear, we visited Doctor D, a Rheumatologist, who noted the "I've had enough of this," attitude. He ordered hemoglobin blood tests and EKG for the heart. He ruled out the possibilities of Neurosarcodosis. Doctor M, the neuro-surgeon we had visited, was now ready to do a Steriotactic brain biopsy of the right cerebella area. This was to be done with an x-ray guided approach, a procedure that she had rarely performed in the cerebellum. This came about after Thanksgiving, on the 26th of November. We do not even remember the thanks of the annual gathering. We were all about the surgery with such intensity that the anesthesia was the only relief. My wife sat with our minister's wife, who is also our minister, for the three hour procedure, waiting and trying to pass the time praying. My wife was intensely preoccupied, wanting to scrub up and take a peek at what was going on in the operating room.

After the procedure I was given a steroid drug, the terrible steroids, to decrease the inflammation from the surgery in the brain. The concern is always seizures, from the invasion of the needles that took five swipes of the Cerebella tissue for observation. My blood pressure was elevated 153/78, high for me due to the fact I'm usually 120/60. I had staples in my head, after that biopsy, and they were removed by Doctor N. My gait could have used improving, but I was able to use a walker. I noted my right ankle was forever swollen.

The right side of the cerebellum controls the right side of the body, unlike the cerebrum that affects the opposite side, i.e., right affects the left and vice versa. My blood sugar took a huge leap upward, as this is another side effect of the steroids, and I was cruising around at the 186 level and normal is 110. Luckily, we were able to get it under control without taking insulin. The brain biopsy was viewed by lab pathologists. They were able to rule out ADEM, as well as Multiple Sclerosis. My wife did not know whether to laugh or cry, she just wanted closure at this point.

On December 9th I was able to walk without my walker. We thought maybe we had a diagnosis by a big university. They wanted to call my problem: Lymphatoid Granulomatosis . . . . how about supercalafragelisticespialadocious. On Dec. 21st we noted that my right leg did not have very good control with flexion, only extension. We faxed out thoughts to Doctor B, a neuro pathologist, and we sent Doctor S of the MAYO clinic in Minnesota, our biopsy slides. We were not satisfied with the findings. We found out that Doctor J in Maryland had a book on Lymphatoid Granulomatosis and was also a pathologist, so a slide of the brain biopsy was sent to her and she was very amicable, and willing to correspond via e-mail. She believed that we should consider Lyme disease, a thought that we had thrown out since we had a negative ELISA test from the get go.

January 28th had arrived and we found my Ataxia to be worsening, and we were nowhere with a real diagnosis. In Feb, our neurologist in Fremont decided we needed low dose orals. So 37.5 mg of Prednisone was administered daily into March. Physical therapy was initiated to help with my gait. We returned to Doctor G to revisit the idea of Multiple Sclerosis and he looked at five MRI's of my brain to compare. In April, doctors reported that they did not note lymphoma or tumor, neither Whipples nor Sarcoid, and the Prednisone oral dose was reduced to 30 mg/day. I was still tired.

April came and depression was obvious, and Prozac was started at 10 mg/day for a week. In May, the docs increased the Prozac to 20mg/day due to no change in affect. The Prednisone was decreased to 25mg/day, a significant amount none the less. Physical therapy was continuing and coordination drills and large rubber ball were used to help me with my balance. Tai chi was recommended, but I just could not muster up the courage for the challenge. By June the steroid dosages were being weaned down to 20mg/day. My 6th MRI of the brain showed marked improvement. The big day came for our eldest son's graduation from high school, and the hallmark moment was my spill off the chair. This would mark the beginning of my dislike for public outings.

We informed our neurologist about the fall and he ordered Imuran, which is also an anti-inflammatory drug, usually given to decrease the amount of those nasty steroids that give so many side effects. The concept that nerves heal at 1 mm/day was comforting until we learned that the slower healing was at the core of the brain and not just the sheath or outside of the nerve. We had a big trip planned to Lake Rollins, in northern California, with a group of friends we had known since growing up in Fremont. I fell again taking a big step, as my right leg was extremely weak. Marcia had to drive the ski boat and I was only able to observe. We came home on the 27th and I was shakier and had wheel-like indents in my tongue on the right. They did not bother me, but they were strange. We also decided to see an eye doctor, as my vision was getting fuzzy. Doctor D. noted a cataract in the right eye.

Our sons were taking a back seat to our blasted doctor visits and unknown findings. Doctor N requested a scan to see if we had a tumor. PET scans would be able to identify a "hot spot." Due to the tongue involvement, we were questioning Bechet's, a rheumatology disease. We almost wished for it just to have a diagnosis. I ended up getting a biopsy on my tongue by an ear nose and throat doctor in his office. He gave me a shot of Novocain and filleted my tongue. Ouch! We visited another ophthalmologist next, and found cataracts to be present in both eyes. I also was deemed not fit to work.

We revisited the notion that I may have a cancer of sorts, even to the point of experimentally giving Cytoxan, a chemo drug, that would wipe out a lot of my cells, good or bad. I was feeling numbness and tingling in my fingers and again steroids were the answer. I had three days and three grams of steroids intravenously. Buzzed, I was. Red dots were appearing on my face and scabby skin stuff on areas. Could it be more side effects from the steroids, or some weird disease process we were not aware of. No one could offer a guess. Our main neurologist decided to take us off any unnecessary drug. I volunteered to stop the Prozac, as I felt the side effects from the anti-depressants to be "depressing", and I really was no longer depressed anyway. Slowly, we weaned me off of steroids by gradually lowering the milligrams weekly. I continued using the walker around the house, as Marcia went on her annual "Girls Wild Weekend." She looked forward to the break, while I anxiously made sure she had all of my help lined up. I do not think the girls were wild, as they were happy for the reunion, and a chance to be women, able to gab freely for hours on end.

Another MRI was scheduled for October and my Prednisone milligrams (mg) were down to 3.2mg a day, almost nothing compared to the 60mg tablets I had started with. I was still taking chemo treatments and was on my third intravenous infusion for the week, when I had a fall on my back. The pain lasted several days. We then contacted our Physical Therapist for a new four wheel walker, after the X-ray of my coccyx proved no fracture. The 7th MRI findings were better than the previous two, so this was encouraging. Doctor G, the specialist of Multiple Sclerosis, had ruled out this possibility, but considered Whipples in the central nervous system.

We had a debate going amongst institutions. The hospital where my wife worked was very intrigued by my disease process. One of the doctors thought I was suffering from a lymphoid inflammatory process, and another neurologist thought I could still have Multiple Sclerosis, which Doctor G was not willing to confirm. We continued notifying our doctor of my ever changing symptoms, and I had increasing lack of balance and weakness. My wife was describing my symptoms and treatments to any doctor that would listen. We were introduced to an infectious disease doctor to re-evaluate whether I had an infectious process happening. I was still tired.

Our eye doctor noted that my Nystagmus, or jerky eye motion, was in both eyes now. I continued my physical therapy, in-between chemo therapy and appointments. I remember falling off of a step when I went to get my hair cut, I was ok, but the thought occurred to me if I continue falling, my wife would have to take care of a guy with a broken hip or who knows what. Number four Cytoxan was given and my journey with chemo was near completion.

Our eldest son in Chico wanted us to visit, so we went up and decided to attend a church. Both my boys, on either side of me, walked me up the old stairs to sit in a church I had never attended before. People were polite, but I felt awkward.

Back home, the infectious disease doctor had some results for me, a positive Epstein Bar virus test. She said it was possible that I had been exposed, but that I was not active with the virus. Oh what good is all this testing anyway! We were determined to finish the course we started, so #5 Cytoxan was given intravenously in late November. My balance was worse, so our doctor ordered another PET scan to determine if anything had changed in my brain. I could not believe my wife actually got hold of someone at the MAYO clinic on the 31st of December. They had seen the slides of my brain and were not impressed with the specimen, and said they were inconclusive. We told the pathologists from the hospital that had originally sent them, and they added an addendum due to the fact they wanted a confirmation of Lymphatoid Granulomatosis. The gram stains were negative for a fungus and grade I EBV was negative on the brain tissue, but this does not rule it out.

A panel discussion encouraged infusion of Interferon Alpha 2B. We were ready to have my eyes measured for cataract surgery thanks to the steroid infusions that quickened the process. Was not this to be for an older person to have, not a 50 year old? They decided to do my right eye first. After the surgery, I was 20/20 without glasses and could see quite clearly. Ah, a success, though I did need to use glasses for reading. In the meantime, my PET scan for cancer was normal, so no cancer.

In Jan. 2003, Doctor W, in Palo Alto, assessed Lymphatoid Granulomatosis and approved treatments with Alpha Interferon 2B. This would be given in subcutaneous injection sites all over my arms, legs and stomach.

I fell on my shoulder and could not move my right leg very well on February first. We kept raising the units of the Interferon injections and they had warned us I would get flu like side effects, and I did. I kept taking the injections even though I was scheduled for surgery on my left eye for the cataract on March 28th. The surgery was successful, but I had to put drops in my eye for a week after. When the units of Interferon reached 15 million I became extremely tired, wobbly and experienced nausea and vomiting. We continued the Interferon at a lower dose.

Of course, the normal dental problems happen, and I needed a root canal. At this point, I wanted to sleep and not go to appointments. They prescribed penicillin to me after the root canal for four days. My wife noted that if I had Lyme disease, one of the treatments was penicillin, although, it would have required a much longer time of dosage.

I was still on Interferon in May when I started occupational therapy for my speech, eating and everyday living management. I was done with Interferon daily injections on May 26th. Four months of the injections and I just could not take it anymore. Plus, I did not get better, just weaker and sleepier. Then to top it off, I developed an infected ingrown toe nail, and was told to soak it with Epsom salts.

On June 19th a central catheter line was placed for Plasmaphoresis. This was done in an effort to "clean" my blood, kind of like they do with dialysis patients, but I would be given 3.5 liters albumin exchange for five days. I took another antibiotic for my ingrown toenail, amoxicillin. Another "illin" to do the job. Interestingly enough on July 11th, #8 MRI showed decreased inflammation in the cerebellum (most improved), but the brainstem continued to be inflamed.

What is up with my injuries? I cut my right toe and was given Augmentin for 5 days. We started getting alternative again on July 21st, as we visited a homeopathic doctor, recommended by a friend at my wife's work. She started me on Shark cartilage capsules and Arnica, used for tissue injury. At this point, we were dropping the steroid usage to 2.5mg. I felt mentally better but my physical ability was still uncoordinated and slow. We went back to the homeopath and she ordered; Phosphate of Ca, Na, Fe, K, Magnesium, and anti-trauma tabs. I was still tired.

My wife was headed on her annual Wild Girls Weekend in October, in Arizona. She found an article in a magazine about a girl with Babesia infection from a cross infection. She realized I may have a tick borne infection, and that not all tick pathogens are the same. We made an appointment on the 24th of October to see a Lyme literate doctor in S.F. He happened to have a cancellation and we went to meet him. I was told to get the Western Blot test and three antibodies were found, indicating I was exposed to a Lyme pathogen. I understood that all I needed was two antibodies to be considered infected and I had three.

He ordered two GM IV Rocephin for two or three months. On December 29th our neurologist agreed to start Rocephin at two grams a day to be given slowly over 10-15 minutes intravenously. Since I would be having my wife give this to me daily, they decided to put a pic-line in me. This is a percutaneous infusion catheter for long term use. On Dec. 31st, we reduced my steroid intake to 12.5 mg/day, and we lowered the dosage 2.5mg every two weeks. Another antidepressant, Paxil, was decreased to 10mg/day, even though I think I was feeling fine. At this point, I decided to stop walking for fear of greater damage to myself. I chose a wheelchair existence, unless all the treatments would change that.

On Jan 4, 2004 at 5 a.m. my right upper chest pain with inspirations, made me think I was having a heart attack. My wife thought it was a pulmonary embolism due to the pic-line, so we called 911. The ambulance drivers came promptly and used their gurney to get me out of the house, such commotion. Doctor R assessed me and gave 4 mg of morphine and 12.5 mg of Phenergan for nausea. Liver enzymes, chest x-ray, CBC, and I did have a temp of 101.5. They x-rayed the pic line and noted it was kinked and straightened it, but did not feel it was sufficient reason for the temperature. We spoke with our Lyme literate doctor and he explained Herx-heimer reactions. These reactions can happen after anti-infectives are given and raise the temperature. This is a good response.

A letter for compensation was written due to the fact the Center for Disease Control had published in 2002 new guidelines for the Western Blot to be utilized for Lyme disease protocol rather than the ELISA test. The Cytoxan and Prednisone most likely exacerbated the Lyme problem. Another hospital would not consider Lymphatoid Granulomatosis and asked us to consider Lyme disease. The ELISA test is only 60% effective. We were reimbursed for some of the fees, as we paid (over $3400).

Prednisone was stopped in March, and I had 64 days of Rocephin with no huge change, other than I felt more uncoordinated. I was still tired. The doctor in S.F. wanted me to take Zithromax, due to spirochetes that may be in white blood cells. I tolerated Zithromax well, but nothing changed.

Doctor N wanted me to stop Rocephin, as he was skeptical about Lyme disease and thought I should try steroids again. Then, as if to show disagreement, I vomited all night and was incontinent. I also had stomach pain.

In June, an ultrasound of my gallbladder was given. For my stomach pain, I got Pepcid, 20mg/day. I had gallstones. We did nothing, as any pain had passed. My urine was darker, but I had no pain. I saw another doctor, and out came the gallbladder. More staples.

In July, Doctor N stated Doctor H, back east, would be a good one to view my case and he suggested we give 1 gram of Steroids, four times for 1 week. I reluctantly agreed. Doctor

K okayed Rituximab infusions and Doctor S concurred better Rituximab than steroids. Infusions of Rituximab were given. I was wobbly and weak, and I wanted to be fed. This was bad.

In late Aug., we decided to buy a friend's van, with a lift. We were able to travel to Marysville, Ca. to an alternative medicine seminar with Doctor B. This was the first time we had been out of Newark in a couple years.

We met with Ed B, a Marriage and Family Counselor, who told us we needed to recalibrate. He talked to us about grounding ourselves, and finding an "eddy" to focus on stuff that stops us. He brought his brother-in-law over, Doctor M, head of Neurology at a major university, for an assessment. It was a wonderful house call. He said he had nothing better to offer than Lyme disease, as far as something that is actually treatable. His words, "Go till the door shuts."

Doctor S, head of a neurology department, suggested I reduce the steroids to 250 mg via an IV, as I was experiencing euphoria big time, and was taking 125mg of Solumedrol, another form of steroid.

In Dec. my wife spoke with Doctor K, of New Mexico, an alternative medicine kind of guy. He spoke of a RIFE machine. This is a great conspiracy story. Doctor Rife was supposedly able to cure cancer in the 1930s. Supposedly, he had built an electron micro-scope that could see cancer cells. He invented a machine that would kill cells at certain frequencies. Big pharmaceutical companies supposedly did not like this. He died mysteriously, and most of the microscopes he had built were destroyed in a fire. To date, only one microscope remains. We bought a RIFE machine from a nice man back east and used it.

At my next MRI in April, the swelling in my brain had gone down. The doctor wanted to know if we had done anything different. We told him about the RIFE machine, but he, being a conservative doctor, chalked it up to coincidence. He did say, however, to keep doing what I was doing.

I had stopped all drugs by now, though I was still very dependent. I was no longer as tired as before. The doctor suggested I go to a rehab place an hour away. This was for three weeks in August 2005 and I agreed, though I was not sure I could do it. The therapy was great, and changed my life. I learned how to get into my chair alone, and how to dress myself. I became more independent, and could use the computer, too. Now, I am up at 8:15 AM, where before it was 10:00 AM. I look at the computer and read the newspaper, where before I did very little. Fear gripped me at the thought of going to the bathroom by myself. My oldest son was home at Christmas and figured out how I could make it work. Now, I can do it by myself. I grab a bar and can make the transfer on my own. This has been the most important thing to happen-major independence. My wife can now leave and run errands, knowing I will be okay.

MRI's are still a part of my life, but only once a year, and after many years, there is still no swelling in my brain. My doctor said things probably would not change much. Who knows what plans God has for my life? I just carry on.

Things have been stable over the last few years, but I still would like my balance back. We went to see another doctor, in February 2012, which we had seen a few years before. He supposedly was more Lyme disease literate and he said I was stable, and that things probably would not change too much. I think he was surprised I looked as good as I did. I was not as impressed this time at his input, as I have stabilized and nothing new was happening. He wanted to do some more blood work and we said fine. There were no big changes, so we just carry on for now.

MORE THAN A CAREGIVER

B efore I tell you what my wife chooses to do, a little history is in order. I first met my wife at our church. Her father was helping on staff, and his wife and four children came to church on Sundays. I had just graduated from high school and became friends with her brother, Mark, who was a year younger than I. The family had returned from the mission field in South America, and he had been doing secular work for a number of years. I met my wife through her older brother and I thought she was just another high school girl at that time. She went to the local Young Life meetings on Monday nights, and it just so happened that I was a leader there. My church helped sponsor me at a missionary conference in Urbana, Illinois in December, 1976, and my wife went, too. We went on our first date in April, and her brother and his wife were supposed to come along. They could not make it, but we went anyway. We went on a motorcycle ride to a Christian camp on the coast, about 40 miles away. We started dating seriously in the fall, but broke up for a few months, and then got married in July of 1980.

I started getting ill in May 2001, and my wife took me everywhere to get tests. It seemed like we were going to different places every day. My wife was on a mission. She had to know what the problem was. All I knew was that my fine motor skills were slowly getting worse. I could still write and walk, but even that was declining. My wife was now driving everywhere, and I used to be the main driver. My wife was a good driver, but I felt like I had to be in the driver's seat. Now, she is taking me everywhere, and I am used to it. Directions can sometimes be a pain, so between the GPS we got for Christmas 2010, and the computer directions, we seem to do pretty well. Plus, my wife calls me her GPS, because I am pretty good with directions also.

Imagine helping someone for a few days. No problem, right? But Marcia does it every day. She lays clothes out in the morning, and then gets breakfast. If she has to work that day, she lays it all out, including meals, at 5:30 in the morning. Cutting things is hard for me. If I were to cut things, they might end up a long ways away, so Marcia cuts things for me. This is not cool. So if we are at a restaurant, I try to order things that I can eat with a fork, and that usually works well.

I usually work on the computer until lunch time on week days, and then I eat lunch and read the paper. I take the weekends off, but the meals still come. A few times a year, I have doctor or dentist appointments, and Marcia drives and waits patiently. She also takes me to an indoor pool twice a week, and afterwards helps me with a shower. Needless to say, Marcia does it all; I think she is a saint. She spends a few nights a year with her girlfriends, while my younger son helps me. One time they went to Lake Tahoe and Marcia had to drive a boat around the lake. She was the only woman with boat driving experience. She had pulled me water skiing and she was a good driver. Things worked out at home while she was gone, but many more days might be hard. It is fortunate that my son lives close by to help when needed.

Marcia works at the local hospital three days a week. She has been there over 20 years and most of the nurses, doctors, and workers respect her. She works hard and has a positive attitude. Many of the people know her situation and do not understand her positive attitude. She has a deaf son and a disabled husband, but keeps on going. I do appreciate all the things she does, even though sometimes I cannot keep track of it all. I can do many things, but I take so long that Marcia usually does it. She knows that God is helping her through everything, and that all will work out, in this life or the next.

One Christmas, a doctor Marcia works with was not going to get a tree because his father was dying and he just did not feel like it. Marcia got him a tree and had it delivered. The wife was very thankful, and knew that she and her husband had been helped by a friend. One never knew when Marcia was going to come up with an idea that would help somebody. She and a friend decided to give a gift certificate at a local restaurant to a couple whose baby was not doing well. We loaned money to a nephew to pay off his car. I could go on and on, she is always coming up with things to make peoples' lives better. The conservative guy that I am, I have to stop her sometimes from giving too much.

Since I do not speak too well, my wife gets most of the telephone conversations. If something needs to be straightened out, my wife is the one who gets to do it now. Before I used to do it, but now my wife is in charge and is much better at any problem solving that goes on. She was on the phone a lot with our local colleges, trying to get our deaf son in a four-year program. The deaf have a hard time because they usually do not speak, so my wife was trying to be his voice so he could get accepted at a local four-year college. He has his two-year degree, but wants a four-year degree. It will help him in the long run to get a job and be more self-sufficient.

We have also joined the local Young Life committee, and my wife gets to make many calls, since I do not speak well. Whenever we have a fund raising event she makes more calls. She does it willingly, as she wants to see this program succeed.

My wife has really gotten into texting. Instead of making a phone call and talking a lot, she can save a lot of time by texting. She is a real multi-tasker, doing many things all at the same time. The only problem is, sometimes she forgets things, and that is not always good. She is doing so much, it is reasonable to forget a few things, since she is not a very big list maker. To her credit, things seem to work out well much of the time. With her family in the area, there is something always happening. Since her parents live near her work, she sometimes goes over there after work to help out where she can. Her parents are no kids, but they get around very well, and always seem to be helping somebody.

Staying in shape is always a challenge. For many years, my wife and a friend have jogged three to four times a week, and sometimes hit Starbucks afterwords. They also hike up a big hill two to three times a month. The hill is a couple thousand feet high, plus they go at 5:30 in the morning, which is crazy to me. It seems like the best time to go for both of them, but Marcia falls asleep early in the evening while watching TV with me. TV is not the best thing, but I had spent the day on the computer, read the paper, and done other things. So I am ready for a little downtime. During all the morning activity, I am fine. Marcia lays out clothes and has breakfast ready, so things work out well. I am usually reading the paper when she gets home from work. It helps Marcia to have a friend who can help keep her accountable. When the friend is unavailable, sometimes the jog does not happen. Staying in shape is a hard thing to do, so having a partner helps a lot. Marcia is in pretty good shape.

Marcia needs to have a life, so I need to realize that I am not number one all the time. Part of the challenge is to figure out things I cannot do and things I just do not want to do. Many times I just cannot physically do things, so I try to state my case. Marcia is a good listener, so we just have to communicate what it is that we want to do. When I say I cannot, it usually means I cannot do it, not I just do not want to do it. My hands are shaky when doing things like setting thermostats, or trying to read things that are too high. If I just do not want to go somewhere, I try to say why, so Marcia does not think I am a complete hermit. Marcia is usually good at making things work and is very flexible when the need arises

It is important that we get time together. I am terrible at listening when I am doing something on the computer, reading the paper, and watching TV. I need to stop more and listen. However, if I am at the last few minutes of a show, or reading a good article, it is hard to pay attention. I am getting better at muting things, and Marcia is getting better at knowing when it is a good time to say something. If I am on the computer or reading, I try to stop and make eye contact, so Marcia knows I am listening. When we are traveling, there usually is not much silence.

There is always something to talk about, as any silence does not last very long. Marcia is a great talker, and loves to discuss things with me. I do not take the opportunity to talk much, so it is nice when Marcia talks and listens. It is nice to talk about things that need to be done. Marcia does not like to talk much about administrative things, but does realize the importance of maintaining things. We also talk about spiritual issues and we seem to be in sync. Every now and then, we get people coming to our house, and sharing spiritual advice. Marcia simply lays out the gospel and prays that it is taken in. It is easy to get off on all kinds of tangents, but Marcia always comes back to the central issue.

Marcia is much more assertive now. Since I am slow at talking, especially in front of groups, she does most of that for me, and quite well, too. We are called Moses and Aaron, as Moses did not speak too well and Aaron was his spokes piece when needed. Marcia speaks well on her own, but gets to speak for me as well. She was never comfortable speaking in front of a group, but now does it much better.

My wife is also a great hostess. I call her "the hostess with the mostess". We recently had a good minister friend and his wife, from Sacramento, plus, my brother-in-law and his wife, over for the Super Bowl. My wife wanted to move the TV into a bigger room and invite more people. I said there would be too much talking, and I wanted to watch the game, plus the advertisements. I actually won this battle. There was all kinds of good food, and we still had a good time. Whenever friends come over, my wife is always offering something, even if they are only here for a short time.

My wife is more than a caregiver to me. We have had quite a history together and we cherish these times. Things could be better with my physical condition, but we make the best of it and carry on. Doubts creep in, but that is okay, as we need to be challenged about everyday life. Marcia cares for me and loves me more than a caregiver would. I do not know what I would do if she were not here. Life is definitely better with her around.

PLEASE LISTEN TO ME LIKE YOU CARE

Communication is supposed to be simple, right? A simply tells B something, and all is well with the world. Unfortunately, it is not that simple. Entire books have been written on communication. B needs to understand completely what A is saying, and then it is possible that a conversation may take place. Sometimes, this does not happen and the communication gets very confusing. People love to assume, because it takes less time to communicate. Unfortunately, it is not always right and the situation gets even more complex. Feelings can get hurt and the wrong thing may be implied, but time was saved. This is very hard because people are so busy. Most people know that assuming is not the right thing to do, but it is easier. I have a little more time on my hands, but it is still an easy thing to do.

Once, I was sitting in the TV room and yelled about something to my wife. She assumed that I meant one thing and did it. I did not mean that, but that is what happened. I was a little irritated and told my wife that is not what I meant. She was cool that time, but sometimes it is a little different. She gets so busy doing things that it is not always easy to do things that I yell to her. I probably need to evaluate my request, but I find it easier this way, and many times that is wrong.

Have you ever been sitting down and talking to someone and their eyes look right through you? You think they are listening, but then you realize that they are not. Are they tired of listening to you, or are they just plain tired? I have to say every little detail and sometimes I think people get tired of listening. Somehow, I think my brain wants to make sure everything is clear and understood. My oldest son simply replies in the middle of my sentence and gets louder, if he disagrees. He thinks he knows what I want to say and he wants to get to the issue fast. Unfortunately, I don't think I can help myself when it comes to going on and on. I think I am a little abnormal in this, and I am not sure what to do. I need to work on this. Usually, my wife is tired, as she has been doing a lot of different things, and needs to take it easy. Others, I am not so sure.

I realize that the world does not revolve around me, but sometimes I make what seems to be unnecessary demands. Of course, I do not think they are, but I need to re-evaluate that. For most people it is no big deal, because they are not here 24/7. My wife is though, and usually my kids, when they are home for the holidays. I have been accused of being selfish, but there are some things out of my control and I cannot do them. I have been treated as independent, but I am not.

Sometimes I do need help. I usually cannot install things, and since my wife is electronically impaired, I need to get someone to help. It is not always that easy, depending on the task. I do not want to ask the same person every time, as that is not fair to them. I do not want people to cringe every time I call, thinking I have another request. My youngest son is great, but I cannot always ask him to do things. One good friend installed a bolt on the bottom of my chair that allows me to go in the van and the chair can lock in place. I do not need to have someone help me. Others have volunteered to help, and sometimes we take advantage of it. If it is a big project, a little gift card goes a long way. It is important to let people know that they are appreciated, and hopefully, they will return upon another request.

Did you know that it is hard to carry on a conversation from two different rooms? I am in one room many times, when someone says something from another room. If I can hear it, I yell back. Sometimes I cannot, and neither of us is willing to come into the other's room, so nothing happens. We end up yelling back and forth, until someone comes into the room. Sometimes we yell between two rooms, trying to carry on a conversation. Usually, we are both doing something and do not want to move into the same room. It makes sense, until someone cannot hear what the other is saying. It would be easier if we were in the same room, but that is not always possible, so we yell back and forth.

Again, time is the big culprit. No one wants take the time to put things down, or stop what they are doing and go into the other room to communicate properly. If my wife is doing something in the kitchen, it is not always easy to stop and come into the other room. If I am watching a program, and it is almost over, I do not want to miss the end, so I do not want to go into the other room. Sometimes, we just wait until it is convenient and then we try to hear what the other person is saying. Patience is important here and we usually have it.

One may not be sure of what I cannot do unless I tell them. There is a difference between things I cannot do and things I can do, but do not want to. Unfortunately, it can be assumed that I can do things and vice versa. Again, assuming can get one into trouble. It is easier in the long run to just ask. Sometimes I say things again and again. Some would call it nagging; I prefer to call it reminding. My memory is pretty good, but there are times when I just do not remember things. I want to make sure something is not forgotten, but I can be overbearing at times. Sometimes, my voice sounds grating, but it is usually not on purpose. If I do want to change my voice pitch, I cannot control how it comes out. I have been accused of sounding terrible, but it is out of my control, I think. My deaf son does not care, he just looks at my body language, and I can tell if things are wrong or not. It seems so simple.

The "walk by" is wild. One walks by me while talking and then goes into the other room before I have a chance say anything. If I want to respond, or I cannot hear it, I have to go into the other room, or yell something. This is not very convenient. It is not always done on purpose, but sometimes I am sure it is. It is a clever way of saying what you want to say and not having to listen to me respond. It does take much time to listen, but these days it seems to be very precious. I have time so it does not affect me as much. That is probably part of the problem. I have more time and others do not, and talking to me takes time.

This brings me to my next communication challenge. I am a little uncomfortable when someone stands over me and talks. I would much rather see them sit in a chair across from me, at eye level. Then, I might not feel like they are up there and I am down here. This is my problem, but it can make me feel more comfortable. I want to look into one's face, not up at it. This is not always possible and I realize that I have to be flexible. People are usually not aware of this and it is okay, it is not the end of the world.

Sometimes, people want to make sure of what they are hearing, so they parrot it back. That is fine, but one should not do it all the time. Imagine a person telling you back what they thought they heard for every sentence. It would drive a person crazy. This usually does not happen, but every now and then there comes a person who wants to make sure you understand everything. They are almost too polite, so I just bite the bullet, and try not to talk too much.

One can always ignore me, too. They simply act like they didn't hear me say anything. If they go into another room, than I am really up a creek. Usually, I just repeat myself and go on from there. Once something gets on my mind, I'm hard to put off too much. I would much rather have a person say what's on their mind, I can take it. Being ignored is not something that I like, and I want to be heard, though I need to evaluate my concern. Maybe it is not that big of a deal. People do not want to necessarily stop and listen to me babble on about something. Business seems to be the priority, and I am not sure that is always good.

Counseling can be an important tool. My wife and I did not think we had problems, but we decided that it would be good to see a counselor to see what he observed. We talked to the same man who counseled us before we got married. His wife had been a teacher at a school where I had done Young Life work, and I knew her. He said that we had many challenges, but that good communication would continue to help greatly. We were in a positive rut, but patience was needed. We had some great sessions, and we even included the boys in one of them. It was good, too. The counselor said that we had no glaring problems, that we just needed to continue sharing what was on our minds. A counselor can bring out all sorts of things to talk about that you have not thought of before. Such was our case, and we came away better for it.

ALWAYS THERE TO HELP

One must talk about their family and friends. Most of the family lives nearby, and some have passed away. One of my favorite sayings is, "My father was a Marine . . . . and so was my mother." My father passed away about twenty-eight plus years ago, and my mother just passed away a few years ago. She was 86. My father smoked non-filtered cigarettes from his late teens until he was 57. He also had a high pressure job and drank lots of coffee. He had heart by-pass surgery at 57 and died of a major heart attack at 62. At least he got to see our first son. My parents met in the Marine Corp in southern California during World War II. She wanted to travel, but got stuck in southern California.

At least she met my dad, and for that I am grateful. My father was from Montana and he wanted to go back there and go to college, after the war. He wanted to get a degree in forestry and stay in Montana. Unfortunately, he fell off a house roof and messed up his ankle. They had to come back to California and then live with my mother's parents for a while. My mother was able to get him a job at a bank where she had worked. She worked, too, but stopped after she had children. They had two boys, of which I am the youngest.

My brother, Chuck, and his wife live in Oregon, and we have been up to see them a few times since I was disabled. We also have traveled annually to their house boat at Lake Shasta, California. Chuck thinks of himself as the black sheep in the family. He and my mom and dad did not always agree on things. I learned a lot about what to say and what not to say. We had to go to bed at 8:30 in the summer when other kids were out playing, and it was still light out. He got me into motorcycles and cars and baseball and a little trouble. He joined the Navy just out of high school, as the draft was after him to go to Vietnam.

One time, when I was riding my bicycle home from school in eighth grade, a boy and his girlfriend cruised by in a car that my brother thought were foolish, and I said or did something stupid and he got out of the car and began to chase me. I was close to home, but I had three corners to negotiate on my bicycle. I did not want to get caught, as I thought this guy would hit me. I made it through the first corner, but this guy was getting close, so I went off to the curb on the next corner, as it was too tight. My books were on a clip on the bike and they went flying everywhere, but I did not care at this point. I barely made it home and ran into the house, and told my brother. He went outside and soon they were wrestling. My mother grabbed a belt and started hitting them until they stopped. I now thought even more of my big brother.

I have two boys that were 13 and 16 when all this started. I could still walk, so they did not notice much, except I was home all the time. Later, they remained cool when I could not walk. My oldest son, Nate, went off to college, which was about a 3 hour drive away. He was close enough if there was an emergency, but far enough away to maintain his independence. I think this was a painful time for him. He had lost an active dad, and was not sure how to handle it. He was still very supportive, whenever he was here. He could also be a real pain, too. He thinks I watch too much TV and nag his mother too much. Of course, I say he doesn't know what he was talking about, but he is right some of the time. He is off in Chicago now. He and his cousin are seeking their fortune there. I think Nate holds the record for the most detentions at his Christian high school. Usually, it was for dress code violations, like untucked shirt or no belt. He was, and still is, a funny guy. He was always providing some comic relief for his classmates.

Zac is my youngest son. He is deaf, so that adds to the complexity of the situation. He has been deaf since he was 13 months old. He was a normal, healthy kid and then he fell down, hit his head and got meningitis, and almost died. At the time, I was asking God why this had to happen. However, I knew that being a believer is no guarantee that weird things cannot happen. My wife and I started taking classes at the local deaf school. We found that Zac reacted well to signs, since he was so young. Our older son did not get much attention during this time. He has adjusted well and gets along great with his younger brother. He has not taken sign classes, but he and his brother have their own way of signing to each other. Zac signs with American Sign Language (ASL), and reads lips pretty well, too. I used to sign okay, but now my hands are too shaky, so I do just the basics. My wife is a good signer; I use her sometimes if he does not understand what I am trying to communicate. Zac lives locally with some friends and goes to the local JC. He has an AA degree, but is trying to get into a four year college with a major in Graphic Design. It is difficult for a deaf person to get into college, as interpreters are required and the college needs to pay for them. He drops by occasionally and helps us out. We get along fine. Zac helps out with the local Deaf Young Life club and has a great disposition on life. He is always positive, with a great attitude. Deaf people usually do not consider themselves disabled, just different.

My in-laws live close by, and are always available. They were Christian missionaries in Ecuador in the late 50s and early 60s. Now, my father-in-law is a retired minister at 89 at my church, though he keeps going like the Energizer Bunny. My mother-in-law is great, and is continually trying to help her grandchildren with something. They have four children, two boys and two girls. With this big of a family, there is always a concern somewhere. Problems just do not go away because you are a man of the cloth.

The oldest child of my in-laws is Mark. He loves cars and dogs and movies and old songs and much more. Oh, did I mention he is a minister? He was in the mission field in South America with his family for many years, and has just recently returned to the states. He is at the same church as my father-in-law. He and I are close in age, as are our wives, and our children. He has a boy and two great girls. He does love tangents, though. For example, he will be telling a story about a person and then go off into a number of different tangents. I want to know what happened up front, so it is quite frustrating for me. I often ask, before he goes into tangents, details about the story. We laugh about this, but it can drive me crazy. He and his wife are great.

Next is my wife, Marcia. All I can say is that she is great.

Next is Robert, or Bobert as I call him, who lives in San Diego with his wife. They have no kids, but are nice anyway. We would like to see more of them, especially as his parents get older. There is about 10 year's difference in age between his brother and he. He and his wife were in a band together, so we call them rock stars. His wife sings and he plays the guitar. They are both good, but they did not get the break they needed. So now they get to be regular people.

And then there is Tam. She lives about 15 miles away, with her husband and two beautiful daughters. She was a normal, mischievous kid growing up, and has a good disposition on things now. She was in the senior high group in church that we helped lead. We did all kinds of other stuff together. Once, when she was in high school, we took her snow skiing with a group of Christian singles. The gals were upstairs and the guys downstairs. One night was special, as we were all going out to eat. Tam was hungry though, and had to have some French fries during the30 minute drive. Later, when we started ordering, Tam was too full to order. We laugh about it now, but at the time, I was angry. Tam's husband helped build ramps in my house, so I could get around easier. He is a great guy and has always been very helpful, even before my disease.

Since Mark is now back in the states, he and his family see us often, and also help out where they can. My brother has come down a number of times to do projects. This family is close, and I am lucky to be a part of it. Many families are not close, but this one gets along with relatives, even if there are disagreements. It is nice to see it when people can be civil to one another and it be genuine, too. The relatives are even great, and we see some of them on a regular basis. Part of my journey has brought me closer to these people and it is fine with me.

Friends come and friends go, but many of our friends are still around. We have a big Christmas card list, and if we were to see these people, it would not take long to feel comfortable. Every now and then we see someone whom we have not seen in a long time. In a matter of no time, it seems like we have not seen them for only a few days. We chat and reminisce like we saw each other yesterday. Some friends have drifted, and we do not hear from them anymore. That is okay, too, as it would be difficult to maintain relationships that are not heartfelt. Many live out of state, and out of the country, but with email, it is easy to stay in touch. We have many friends, but like most people, only a few close ones. They live nearby and we see them all the time. One couple has us come over quite a bit, and it helps that I can get into their house easily with my chair. After my disease, our close friends remain close. This has been great for my wife. It is nice to still have friends that one can talk to when needed. This is refreshing. I consider them rocks among sand.

You Mean I Have to Budget?

My parents were depression children, and were really tight with the dollar. My mother was a full-time housewife and my father was a banker. She would also pay the bills, and he would also count the church money once a week. My mother salted enough money away, that we were able to visit her sister in upstate New York, the summer of 1964. She also sold Avon so she could buy a piano. My father took a bus 20 miles to work, until we could afford a second, used, car, when I was in junior high school.

I had to have some spending money, so one of my first jobs out of high school was with a nearby recreation department, in Newark. A friend, who I would later go to Europe with, got me an interview with the boss. It turned out that he once lived down the street from me. He was about five years older than I, and had a sister who was one year older then I. I was her campaign manager when she ran for office in Junior High school. I got the job and the hours worked well with the college classes I was taking. I worked there for a number of years. My boss had gone to a university and was a Viet Nam war veteran. He had been shot and could no longer run, but he got around very well. He was a great basketball player in high school. Now, he can still shoot the ball great.

I met my bosses wife, and he and I actually did a few things together. We took a four-hour drive, one way, to see a comedian named Don Rickles, at Lake Tahoe. Unfortunately, I felt like I was going to have a heart attack, and spent two hours in a room breathing oxygen. I missed the show and we drove home. The next day I went to the doctor and he asked me if I had done anything different. I said no, but a kid was goofing around at a recent Young Life club, and hit me in the chest. He said that I had probably been hit near the heart, and that the increased elevation had made my chest swell and ache. I needed to take a few days and relax. I did, and was all better. I never did get to see Don Rickles. Anyway, with the job, I now had enough money for gas and activities.

All through college, and until I got married, it seemed like I had just enough finances to get by.

Now, things changed. Did we have enough money to live on? "What do you mean, we are out of money? I have plenty of checks," said the spouse. My wife is not like that, but in the beginning of my illness, I was not sure we could live like we were before. I was on short-term disability the first six months that I stopped working. Fortunately, I had about six months of sick leave saved, so we could use it first, and we were able to live and pay bills. Things were very complicated. There were forms to fill out and people to see, so it got crazy.

We never did live high off the hog. We have a small house in an older area. We had two cars and a boat. We got rid of one car and the boat eventually, thinking I might recover. I had grown up water skiing, so I did not want to part with the boat immediately, and my kids agreed. My oldest son was very disappointed that we did sell the boat. We sold it for cash to a friend of a friend. My brother wanted to buy it, too, but I needed the cash immediately, and I was not sure what the financial arrangements would be. After a couple years, a friend gave us the money to buy a used van which had a ramp in it. These things are not cheap. We were very fortunate, and have tried to give most of the money back, now that things are better.

We had some savings, but since we did not want to change much, it went pretty fast. My mother had some money, but we did not want to burden her. Our church helped out with a couple thousand dollars each month, for a few months. We did not want to give up our missionary giving, and this allowed us to pay bills and get by while we were applying for Social Security. Fortunately, I had been paying weekly for long term disability, which I did not think I needed. I thought I would never need it, but did not want to take any chances. It kicked in after six months of short-term disability was over. This gives you 50% of your current salary, less any Social Security benefits, so it was very welcome. To this day, over 10 years, I have received over $200,000 which I would not have gotten at all, had I not taken out this disability insurance. Of course, I had to prove that I was disabled. The doctor had to fill out forms, which was a real pain. We did finally receive the funds.

My wife was working part-time as registered nurse. She was working only two days a week with no benefits. She made good money, and with one son in private school, and one deaf son, the time off was valuable. Now I entered the picture. What was she to do with this weird disease I had? I was okay while I could walk, but then things changed. When I could no longer walk, my mother-in-law helped out. She was great, and even though I could still get around, there were things I still could not do. My mother-in-law is no kid, so eventually we hired a caregiver for days when my wife worked. The man we hired was great. He worked at General Motors and his wife was also a nurse. When General Motors closed down he sold his house, and moved to Patterson, about 1 1/2 hours away. Fortunately, I was a little more independent, and could get by without him. It helped us financially, too. We were now able to afford a new car for my wife that got good mileage, a Toyota Prius. It was good to have a car that she could depend on, since I could not work on it.

I had a retirement plan at work, which I converted to an IRA with the financial advisor. I had been doing business with this man for years, and he helped me out with all the paperwork involved. One of the many stupid things I have done in my life was to take some money out of my retirement plan. In 1998 I wanted a tournament boat for water skiing, but I could not afford one. I took the money out of my retirement plan and got the boat. Since I made an early withdrawal, I was penalized on my taxes that year. I ended up paying a few thousand dollars more than I normally would. This was stupid. Sometimes it is necessary, but in this instance it was not. I had the boat two years before I got sick, so it turned out okay.

My wife now has a retirement plan at her work, and my financial advisor has helped us pick out what she should be investing in. Hopefully, when she retires, we will have enough funds to live, since we both have pensions and retirement plans. If Social Security is still around, we will have that, too.

We pay bills on a weekly basis. We sit down together, get the check book out, and see what we owe. My wife is the check writer and I help with the decisions on what needs to be paid. My wife had not done this before, so she was real nervous at first. She has it down now and does a good job. We have a budget and have to be careful with the credit cards. It is easy to charge, since no money is required. We have an account on Amazon, and it is very easy to get carried away on the computer. We have to be careful about things that we buy, even if it is a good deal.

It is hard to believe that our first house in 1981 was $86,000 at an interest of 10%. This place had only two bedrooms, one bathroom, and a one car garage. We added on after we had one child and a second one was on the way. We had some contractor friends who were able to help us do the addition. I even got to do a lot of work, too. Since we did not have a lot of money, this really helped. Two bedrooms and a bathroom were added. Now we have three bedrooms and a TV room.

This worked out well. We refinanced a couple of times and finally got a 15 year loan at a much lower rate. We rented the first year, but realized we needed to invest our money and we were ready for a home. My dad did not like the area and offered to pay us $1000 not to take it. He and my mom did help with the down payment though, so we knew my dad really had our best intentions at heart. We still live here, and enjoy the area, so it has worked out pretty well.

When my mother passed away, she left me some cash and an insurance policy. She was a great lady and lived locally for many years. We were able to convert the life insurance policy to me, which was great. I am not insurable now in my existing condition, so this money will go to my wife someday. We gave 10% of the money mostly to our church, paid off some bills, and put the rest in savings. I have a new car fund which I put a little bit of the money into. I like to change my wife's car every few years, so there is less work to be done.

Our house was in pretty good shape when I got sick. We did have to put on a new roof and have done a few other small projects. A contractor friend and a bunch of Young Life people were able to put on our new roof at a greatly reduced price. We knew a good handyman, too, and he was able to do many little projects that were important.

Now, my sons have moved out, my wife works 3 days a week with benefits, and our house is paid off. Things change, but we still have bills. Finances are important and one has to stay on them continually. We are fine financially, but with this crazy economy one never knows what is going to happen next.

7

WILL THEY BE AROUND, PLUS

One always wonders if people will be around after a crisis. In this case, the body of believers was there. I had grown up in this church since 1955, and I was 4 1/2. My father became an elder, and the church treasurer. I was an elder too, three different times, for a total of nine years. The first time I was in my early 20s, and did not really know what was going on. I worked part-time here for a year while I was going to graduate school. I ran the Youth Club, which was an after school program for fourth through sixth graders. But that was many years ago, and I was not sure if people would respond. The current head of staff and his wife came and visited for years. When they first came to the church in the 90s, my wife and I took them to San Francisco, since they were from southern California. We got to know them well. I had known every pastor at our church since high school and I wanted to know these folks, too. My wife's father was now on staff, so once a year we would go up to Lake Tahoe during Thanksgiving, to spend time with the staff and their families. We got to know the staff really well, too.

One senior minister had been at our church 20 plus years, and he was a good friend. He was a great preacher, but lacked in administrative skills. He was very conservative, but did not have a political bone in his body, in regards to the church workings. One of the other ministers was great with administrative things, so it was a great team. He left, however, and he was replaced with another good man. Unfortunately, in my opinion, he got in with a group that was negative towards our senior minister.

After a lot of discussions by members, the Presbytery made a ruling that both ministers had to leave. They could go to another church, but they had to leave this one. Many were in shock, but the ruling stood. The senior minister worked in various churches in California as an interim minister. The other minister went to Texas. It was a small world when the senior minister's daughter went to church in Texas and saw this associate minister there. She decided that particular church was not for her. Politics had sunk a good man, and I still have not forgotten it to this day. The current minister and his minister wife then came, and they have been here over 10 years. He is a good speaker, and also has good administrative skills. The wife knows her stuff, and is really involved.

My wife and I also taught classes in the early 90s for Parents Under Pressure (PUPs). I said it was supposedly a class for people whose lives had gone to the dogs. We would discuss various spiritual and real-life topics. We would try to teach various theological issues in 45 min. We did that just to get people interested in the topic.

Ever wonder why cults who come to your door seem to go all over the place, or focus on an interesting topic? They tend to know their Bible better than us, but I think it is usually interpreted incorrectly. It is usually best to focus on Jesus. I used to have things all written up, in case someone came by to witness. I would usually conclude by saying, "Either you are right, or I am right, or we are both wrong". Based on what was being said, we could not both be right. My notes helped me to focus on what really mattered. Needless to say, the class was very challenging.

Meals came our way four and five times a week. It was a good break for my working wife, and we did not get just casseroles, even though they were good. This did not just keep up for a few months, but many years. We had to cut that down to two days a week, and then finally said, "Enough is enough, stop being so nice." We felt very blessed that the body of believers would come to our aid.

When we needed help paying bills, the deacon's fund was there helping us. They gave us thousands of dollars, until we could get our feet back on the road. To this day, we give money to the deacon's fund, because they were there when we needed help. People we did not know became friends, all because they wanted to serve. One couple rode motorcycles, but he was in an accident and could no longer ride. They have since moved to Florida. Another lady brought her daughter, who became friends with our dog. Another woman was a stewardess, who I had known in high school. Another woman was a mom who we did not know. We had all types of different people delivering meals.

A couple different work parties came over to our house to fix things and clean up. We live in a house that was built in 1948. House lots were different then, ours was 50 feet wide and 150 feet deep. There was always something that needed to be done. My wife was not exactly a fixer upper, so this was very timely. We did not know some of these people, but they came all the same. Some of the bulbs they planted still come up every year. People still ask if there is something they could do to help us. This has meant a lot to us.

I do not go to church, but I still listen to CDs on Sundays. I just do not feel comfortable going, as my voice is slow and people want to talk. Plus, I have bathroom issues in the mornings. We meet with five other couples once a month at different houses that can handle my chair, to discuss various spiritual topics. These are people I have known for years, and are around our age. One couple would drive about 30 miles, because they used to go here. I used to play softball with this guy, and his wife is a nurse like mine. I played basketball and softball with another guy, and he bought ramps for me to access his house, and they are not cheap. One woman was on a committee that I was on, and we got along well. Plus, her husband is cool. One man and his wife used to come to our classes many years ago. We knew the other couple just from going to church, and I played basketball with him at church, and she is also a nurse. Their daughter also went to the same college as my older son. We always have something to talk about.

I have gone to a few funerals at my church. There is always somebody there who I know and we talk for a little while. I am much more comfortable talking to someone while they are sitting down, looking me in the eye. We always seem to be close to the last ones to leave. I think it is because my wife has always loved to talk.

My concept of tithing came from this church. The bible says at least 10% is to be given away, but I think the national average for Protestants is more like 3%. This seemed sad to me, so I wanted to give away at least 10% of my earnings, but this all happened after I was married. One of our ministers, who is now deceased, had 10% taken off the top of his wages. Things were tight, so we decided to give 10% of my income to the church and some of my wife's income to missionaries we knew. Today, we give away at least 10% of any income. I first started giving money to a gal that was a friend I knew from Young Life leadership, who was joining a college ministry called Collegiate Encounter with Christ. This was before I got married and I did not give much. I knew more about giving, though, and that was an important step. My wife is a real giver, so we had no problem trying to tithe. Money is much tighter for everyone these days, but ministries still go on. We now give to the church, the local Young Life organization and different outside missionary families we know. It looks good, but I'm sure we could give more.

The church has been an important part of my life. There are spiritual networks to tap into, as well as social groups.

Hopefully, one can be themself, and not a clone, saying all the socially and politically correct things. There is a great song by a Christian singer named Steve Taylor, called "Do You Want to be a Clone". Everyone at a church is telling a new believer how he needs to act a certain way. He could not be himself, but had to behave correctly, according to them. It is bad when we cannot be ourselves.

There was also a lot of spiritual information I received from Young Life. In 1970, I went to see a Young Life club when I was a freshman in college, at the request of a friend. I had been playing college basketball at the local junior college and decided to visit the club. I was amazed that so many kids got together, so I went to a few more clubs to investigate. I liked what I saw, so I joined the leadership.

I went to a summer camp in Canada a year and a half later as a junior counselor. A high school boy asked me a question, and I said I would get back to him soon, as I did not know the answer. After getting an answer from the head counselor, I realized I had made no spiritual commitment myself. I said to myself, "It is either believe, or get off the pot". I chose to really believe in Christianity, and I read more in the next few years than I have in the past 30. A great book by Francis Schaeffer, "Escape From Reason", helped me understand what faith was all about. Then, our paid area staff man took another job, so we kept the club going for one more year, until we got another. The new staff person was a man who was only a few years older than us. He was single, and had graduated from Stanford University. He was sharp, but we like to say we taught him everything he knew. Now, he is in charge of the Asia territory, which is quite large.

I was now a senior leader and was in charge of a club along with a gal senior leader. We used to visit a high school campus without any problem. Now it is very different. Ah, those were the days. My wife and I are still involved in other ways in Young Life to this day.

I Do Not Want To Go

If it involves an airplane, I usually do not want to go. There are bathroom issues to worry about and getting around is not very easy. We went to Argentina as a family to visit my brother-in-law and his family for two weeks in late 2007. It worked out okay, as I did not have to go to the bathroom on the way, or coming back. I lucked out. Getting to and from the seat was a lot of work, and people stare. I did not like it. I did not take the electric chair, so I was in a regular wheelchair being pushed around. Imagine yourself on a steep hill with no control. As I was pushed carefully, I just closed my eyes and held on, praying I would make it. The stories I could tell.

When I was in late elementary school, my dad's idea of a vacation, for a couple years, was driving to Montana for two weeks. He would drive a tractor there most of the time. My mother would get up early, make meals, and do wash. She realized this was not a vacation for her, so we stopped going to Montana. We were never told of the real reason, but I suspect this was it.

At home, we travel around in a van that has been modified to include a ramp. These things are not cheap. A woman friend bought us our first used van, which we have since traded in. We try to stay at a hotel one night a month. This sounds expensive, but it really is not. We have taken the points we get from credit cards and airlines, and use them for hotel overnights. All we pay for is gas and food, depending on where we go. We have been doing this for over five years and have seen a lot of different places. Once, we went to see some friends about 100 miles away. We had dinner with them, and then we went to our hotel and they went to their house, since it was not very wheelchair accessible. It was great. Another time, we saw some friends who lived in the wine country, and we toured the area and then went to their house and talked. It also was great. We have also driven to places where we do not know people, but we manage to see the area and talk to each other.

We usually stay within a few hours of our house, so my wife does not get so tired driving. However, we have made a few overnight trips to my son's college. We do not leave until after I've gone to the bathroom. Going places with the condom catheter has become much easier. I am now not so anxious. Having to go while traveling in a wheelchair, without the catheter, is not so simple. Once, before the catheter, I had to go real bad and my wife just said to hang on for a little longer. I said that if we did not pull over now, we would have a problem. She pulled over.

We also went to San Diego to see my son water ski. My younger son helped drive, so it was easier on my wife. We have been to Portland to visit my brother two times. We took our dog and stayed at a hotel coming and going, explaining she was a help dog for me. It was fine. We went to Colorado to visit some friends for a week during the pre-catheter days. Gas was not cheap, but it was a vacation, right? Timing was important, and we did okay.

My brother has a houseboat on Lake Shasta that we have visited a few times. The houseboat has a bathroom that is for disabled people, so I can use it. Getting onto the houseboat is scary. There is a ramp that I use and I am onboard in no time. Not too many people cruise around the lake in a wheelchair, I feel honored.

I did my share of travel before I was married. I want to mention three, since they were all fairly long trips. First, I went to Europe in 1972 with some friends for eight weeks. Originally, there were eight of us, five guys and three gals. Only three of us ended up going, one gal and two guys. The boyfriend of the gal said it was okay to go, since he was a friend of ours, too. He was originally supposed to go, but had to work. We were going to go on five dollars a day, plus flight and other transportation expenses, and only ended up paying $850 for our eight week trip. This included airfare and a four week first-class train pass.

When we were first in England, we had bought used one speed bicycles, and they seemed fine. Just a few days into the trip, however, the other guy had a bad stomach ache and went to the hospital. We called up to see how he was, and were told that he was just fine, recovering from of an appendicitis attack. It had been removed and he had to stay there and recover for two weeks. There was no cost, but now we had to figure out what to do. We said we would meet him in the South of France in two weeks. After bicycling to Paris and the Loire River Valley we connected up. We were able to sell the bikes to a hostel on the coast of France, but the bicycling before we met him, with one speed bicycles, was a real pain. Big hills were not our friend. We had done a lot of camping, and ate a lot of pastries, and we survived on less than five dollars a day.

Later, we even visited Francis Schaeffer's L'bri Fellowship in Switzerland. This was a well-known Christian conference ground. Schaeffer was not there, but we had lunch with a well-known Christian author named Oz Guinness. We told him we had visited Peninsula Bible Church, which was very well known in the San Francisco Bay Area, a few times. He wondered if the church could survive without the head pastor, who was very popular. It is still going to this day. We had some great conversations and hitchhiked back to the train station.

We had a great trip. We had hit England, France, Spain, Portugal, Morocco, Switzerland, Germany, and Denmark. When we returned, our families were waiting at the airport. I had grown a little chin hair and my dad thought it looked stupid, but he was glad that I was home. I had taken a New American Standard new testament Bible to read, and I still have it to this day. There is even a watermark in the end of John 16, where I got hit by a sprinkler in France.

Second, I went cross country on my motorcycle for seven weeks in 1976. My dad and I had just bought a Honda 1000. Now my dad had never been on a motorcycle before. He had me upgrade from a Honda 160 to a 450, then to a Honda 750, as he had friends selling them. Then I saw a Honda 1000 in the show room on my way to college and he decided to invest in it and learned how to ride a motorcycle. He had a friend who rode, and he decided at the age of 52 that he would too. He said he would help only if the motorcycle had a fairing/windshield. Of course, I said yes. He went on many trips with a suit case strapped to the back of the motorcycle.

I left in the rain and got to see Glacier Park in Montana, but was sick and stayed with relatives in Montana for two days to recuperate. I was driving across Canada when I met a guy going home to New Jersey, who was also on a motorcycle. We drove together until we got to his house in New Jersey. This guy was quite a character. Every morning he would put a six pack of beer on ice in his motorcycle saddle bag. I was good for one, but he would drink the rest throughout the day. He was going to take me to New York City, but spent the last of his money on some marijuana. He and his family were nice, but my lifestyle was different from his.

I had met a girl from New Jersey in 1966 at the Smithsonian Institute in Washington DC, and we had written to each other for quite a number of years. I had been with my family sightseeing and she was a Girl Scout, sightseeing too. My thought was to look her up. She had been married, divorced and was now single, living with her parents. I met her and she was very nice, but I realized that she really was not my type.

Now, I headed back toward California. There was much to see, and then in Colorado I met some other motorcycle people. There were a guy and his girlfriend and another guy, and we decided to travel together. One guy had been to Las Vegas, so when we got there he showed us around. We had good, cheap food, but we were all on a tight budget and camped locally. I made it home and had seen a lot. The scenery was great and I got to see a number of relatives along the way.

Third, after my current/only wife decided she was not ready for marriage yet, I went to South America, in 1979, with Wycliffe Bible translators for 12 months. I did not want to tell Marcia that I was going on the mission field, as I was afraid she would say yes just to be a missionary. We ended up getting married when I returned. Absence did make the heart grow fonder. I was supposed to go to Colombia in September 1978, but there were visa problems. I went to Mexico City in January to learn Spanish while I waited for my visa, which was supposed to come soon. When it got to June, I decided to stay in Mexico. Then, soon after I received my visa. I changed my mind and went to Colombia in early July via Miami.

While I was in Mexico City learning Spanish, I worked in the office doing budgets. I stayed in a 15 x 15 dorm room with a man who was a translator in the western part of Mexico for seven months. He was in his late 50s, single, and came across a little rough at first. I got to know him and he was quite cool.

I worked with the senior high group, too, and went to a secular Spanish school in downtown Mexico City. I met a young German man, in his early 20s, and we became friends. We wanted to climb a local mountain, so one day I spent the night with him and his family, and then we got up at four in the morning. He drove for two hours and then we started climbing at six in the morning. The mountain was 18,000 feet high, and we started at 12,000 feet. We also brought snow clamp-ons for our feet, since the last few hundred feet had snow. We got to the top, looked around and saw clouds coming. We soon started down and it only took two hours. I had borrowed some boots from a high school kid, and they worked fine. The climb was a success. The name of the mountain was Mt. Popocatepetl.

I also met a gal who was engaged to a guy in the states. She was on a short term mission, but met another guy, who was not with Wycliffe, and married him. They stayed in Mexico as missionaries with another organization and are still there today. We support them and get to see them every now and then. There were all kinds of political things happening at that time. The university was near us and many of the students thought Wycliffe, or Summer Institute of Linguistics as it was known, was not good. They said we were changing cultures, but we were only trying to put languages into a written form, and using the Bible as a sample to read. Hopefully, things did not change that much.

The place I went to in Columbia was about 100 miles from Bogotá, in the llanos, or flatlands. I had to be driven to a town called Villavicencia, and then fly to the Wycliffe town called Loma Linda. The road was really bad, so I got to fly or it would have taken a long time to drive. This place was cool, as it had a commissary, an airplane hangar, doctors office, printer building, mechanic building, and a generator building. There were about 50 houses near a lake that had caimon and pirana fish. We were safe though, and could even go swimming. We lived two miles from a town, but this was not a compound. Anyone could come and go as they please.

One day, we had a lot of troops come through our land, looking for rebels. The rebels did not like us, but we stayed anyway, thinking God would protect us if necessary. I worked in the main office doing budgets and I lived with a single guy, in a house not too far from the office. I met a couple whose kids were in ninth and six grade. The sixth grade boy is now a new Wycliffe missionary, and the we support him. We lived close to a man and his wife and daughter, and he was shot and killed a couple years later. He had gone to the group house in Bogotá for a dentist appointment. He was kidnapped and killed by the rebels, who the troops were protecting us from. Loma Linda was later closed down by the government. It was just too dangerous.

Life seemed normal at Loma Linda, and I joined the WUGGs (Wycliffe unmarried guys and gals). On an entertainment night for everyone, we presented a skit that I had learned in Young Life. It was very funny and went off well. On a talent night, the Dan West singers arrived. Myself and four gals lip-synched an old Dan Hicks song. It also was funny, and well-received by the folks.

I also got to fly out to a couple of the many native villages. We were in a short landing and take-off plane, as the landing strips were nothing more than a meadow. One of the man villagers, in a G string, wanted to send back a message to the translator. This was in his own native tongue, and that meant a lot. I now got the picture. People respond much better when they can write in their own native tongue. There are about 6,800 languages/dialects in the world today, and approximately 2,000 have no written form at all. We went to another village, but on the way back we encountered rain clouds, and had to return to the village. We spent the night, and a villager in another G string gave us some fried fish and plantanos to eat. We returned the next morning. I came home in December 1979, just in time for Christmas. I had a great experience during my time away. I could still be with Wycliffe if I had gotten married first.

There were quite a few great trips in my earlier years, and I have just told you about a few. Now, I get to ride around in an electric chair much of the time. It is quite different, but my wife and I still manage to get around. I am still fairly adventurous, I just do not like to fly anymore.

THERE USED TO BE MUSCLE THERE

I used to jog a couple days a week, and play a lot of sports. We used to go water skiing as a family a couple weeks a year. I had been exposed to second hand smoke for a long time, but I also got tons of exercise as a kid. Physical education was required in schools, plus there were no video games, or computers, or Internet. I do not think there would be as much of an overweight problem today if we got a little more exercise. There used to be muscles in places where I no longer have them. Of course, my stomach is a whole lot bigger. My weight went from 175 to 189 pounds. My waist has gone from 33 inches to 39 inches, and it would be more if I was not somewhat disciplined. My fingers and legs have gotten skinnier, but my weight has gone up. Well, things have not changed much, but I have a little more muscle now.

I have had a trainer one day a week for a few years now, and I have worked out on a weight machine for 45 minutes, three days a week the last few years. When this first started, I would walk around a lake with my wife a few days a week. I stopped when I could no longer walk, plus the drugs I was taking made me feel very tired. No, I do not look like Hercules now, but my arms are bigger, and I feel better, too. The trainer is great, plus he is a nice guy. He has a great story, as he was a young boat person from Viet Nam many years ago.

He came over here with a mom and dad and eight brother and sisters when he was nine. They were sponsored by my church and then were broken up to stay with people. He now works at the hospital where my wife works. He got his degree from a local state college and works at the hospital. He has become wealthy, and does not need to work much. The benefits from the hospital are important, since he has two kids. He is a great worker, too. My wife was asking him about the church that he was sponsored by, and he said that it was a ski sloped place. My wife continued asking him about the church, as it sounded like our church. He said that some gray-haired man helped them out at the church and my wife showed him a picture of her father. He said that was the guy. Divine.

Moving to and from an exercise machine is hard, but it is doable. Since I had no balance and my legs were shaky, having stronger arms made all the difference. One can do all kinds of different things. I can now transfer from one place to another much more easily. Since my oldest son figured out how I could transfer from my seat to the toilet on my own, my wife has more independence, and so do I. She can take off, and I am fine. My boys can actually see and feel the difference in my arms. The shakes are still there, but I am more confident.

I have been going to a local indoor pool twice a week. They are set up for handicapped, so they have a chair that puts you in the water and lifts you out. I usually walk for one half hour, holding on to the side, and do some exercises for 15 minutes. I wear a safety belt, just in case I lose my balance, which has only happened once in 5+ years. I do not want the life guard to have to jump in for me all the time. My wife sits near the life guard and has some great stories. One gal was going to be a Marine. Others would share their life story, it was very interesting. Everybody knows me now. I provide a little excitement for the lifeguards, since they really have to keep their eyes on me to make sure all is well. Hopefully, I help break up the monotony of watching all the time.

I do about 15 minutes of exercises in bed 3 days a week. Lie in bed and do exercises—something does not sound right. I actually do stretches, arches and modified stomach crunches. Sundays are for doing nothing, as it gives me something to look forward to. Also, I do some AB exercises out of bed for about 15 minutes. If you add all this time exercising up, it is not very much. However, a body does not require all that much to keep it in reasonable shape. It helps to be consistent, too.

A friend of my wife used to come by every two weeks and give me an hour long acupressure massage. This went on for a couple years. It was great, and free, too. We gave her a Starbucks card every now and then as a thank you, but we probably should have done more. Scheduling got to be difficult, so we had to stop. Too bad.

Since August 2009, I have used an exercise bicycle three days a week, 30 min. at a time. Getting on the thing is a real pain, but I manage. There is an attachment place for an iPod, which I use so it is not so monotonous. There are about 800 songs that shuffle, so I do not hear the same song too often. I try to work up a good sweat. Sometimes I even have to change shirts. Our dog used to come by and lay down next to me, but now she has passed away, so I get to do it all by myself. It is not something I look forward to, but I need to do it. My blood pressure has gone down, thanks to this work out. I went to the doctor recently and my blood pressure was

103/60, which was very good. I assume it is also because I was very athletic all my life.

Diet is important. I try to eat three meals a day and have plenty of liquids. Vitamins are important, too. I am not taking any drugs, but I am taking pills like calcium and vitamin D and fish oil and regular vitamins. Every now and then I have to have an In-and-Out hamburger. We do fast food once or twice a week, and try not to eat too much. We mix it up, and actually have some healthy things. We recently went with some friends to a restaurant in Santa Cruz. It had a gondola car that I had to ride in, in order to get to the restaurant. I barely fit in, but we made it, as it would only take six people. With me, it was my wife and I only. Portion control helps, and my wife helps make sure that we eat right most of the time. I had cucumber sandwiches once, and they were okay, but I will take a hamburger or a piece of pizza over them any time.

Like many people, I like chocolate. If I eat a lot, though, that is not good, so I have to be disciplined. It would be very easy to gain a lot of weight, because I really do not do that much, physically. I do not have seconds, and try not to snack too much. A beer is consumed once in a while, and every now and then I will have a little single malt scotch. I used to go to Scotland once a year on business, and would drink more in one week then I did at home all year. After 10 years, I could actually drink scotch without ice and add only a dollop of water. I would like to blame a certain Scotsman, but that would not be true. I took my wife over two times and we became friends with the man and his wife. When they came over here, we had them over for dinner a couple times. We were going to go to San Francisco, but the traffic was bad, so we went to a restaurant nearby. It was a little rustic, but they did have some soccer/football games on TV that he enjoyed. Since then, the place has expanded even more and the food is good, too. Since my disease we still keep in touch on the Internet. Anyway, the key to food and drink is moderation, and my wife is a great dietician, too. I even get dessert sometimes. A proper diet and good exercise help me stay reasonably fit.

❦ 10 ❧

I Used To Just Do It Myself

I f something was not being done, I used to just do it myself. Now, it is not that easy. I might have to wait, or it is possible that it will not get done at all, although I am quite persistent. When my older son is home, he takes his time doing things, so I never know when something is going to get done. This drives me nuts. There are some things that I just am not physically able to do, so this can be very frustrating. I am much more concerned about minutiae than my wife. I am usually Mr. Symmetric, and this can drive my wife crazy. If I have a list of things to do and my wife has a list of things to do, it cannot all be done. A few things can be done by me, but most of it needs to be done by my wife.

Since it cannot all be done by my wife, my nearby youngest son does a few things, but he too cannot do it all. Sometimes, we hire a handyman, but there are still little things that need to be done. Since I have a little more time on my hands, I am constantly reminding my wife of things that need to be done. She rolls her eyes and usually does it. If it is something that cannot be done by her or I, it is time to call a friend or a handyman.

I used to be a smooth speaker. Now, my speech is slow, and sometimes it is hard to understand me. Before, I did not mind speaking in front of groups. Once I was reading Scripture in church and I said "Eat drink and be Larry", instead of, "Eat drink and be merry". I was only joking, since Larry and I are good friends, and he attends the same church. Saying this in church might not have been the best idea, but I wanted to know if people were listening. They were, and many laughed, since they knew that Larry and I had a strong relationship. I still wonder about this. Now, I do not like talking a lot if the group is larger than six. I will only say a few things instead of a lot of things in a large group. It must be pride, and I am having a hard time dealing with this.

Getting up in the morning used to be simple. I would get up, put on a some clothes, and go about my business. This took a couple minutes. Now it takes 10 or 15 minutes. It is no longer easy to get up and get dressed, like it used to be. By the time I get dressed, and transfer myself to my chair, a lot of time has passed by. This has to be done every morning, seven days a week, 365 days a year. I am used to it now, but it does get frustrating, and then I have to get in bed at night, too.

Going to a restaurant can be great, but it can be a pain, too. Sometimes, the table is too low, and I cannot get under the table unless I put my feet on the ground, lifting up the foot plate. This can be done, but again, it is very frustrating. I try to pick things that my wife does not have to cut, but she still ends up helping me a little. A straw is necessary to drink water, and the waiters are always accommodating. Eating out is usually nice, but I will get a few stares from patrons. I just block it out and go about my business.

Going to the bathroom can be very intimidating. I cannot take my time, or bad things can happen. Going out in the morning before I have gone to the bathroom is something I usually do not do. This is not always convenient, especially if we are spending the night in a hotel. However, I would much rather wait, then have an accident in the car. If I am watching the end of a show, reading an interesting article, or at the computer, I have to immediately give it up and go to the bathroom. Going tinkle is easy, as I can stay in the same place and use a plastic urinal. Every now and then I need help from my wife in the bathroom, but that does not happen often. It has taken some time to learn all these things, and all I can say is, listen to your body.

Financial matters can be a problem, too. Fortunately, my wife is good at handling things. Every now and then, a situation arises requiring us to think hard about a bill. I cannot speak very well on the phone, so my wife usually does the talking. If I do talk on the phone, I first say that I am handicapped. People are much better at listening if they know the other person is handicapped. They have to listen well, in order to understand what I am saying. This is not easy, though, it usually works out well.

The market goes up and then the market goes down. It is hard to plan actual retirement when these things happen. I have an IRA, long term disability and Social Security right now. My wife has a retirement plan and a pension building up. When I officially retire, I will have the IRA, a pension and hopefully, Social Security. When my wife retires, she should have her retirement plan, a pension and hopefully Social Security. We should be okay, unless the market decides to take a dive.

Unfortunately, money is important. I remember back in 1986, we were wondering how we could afford two cars, and we needed them. My wife was working part-time and pregnant. Plus, we were adding on, as two rooms and a bathroom just does not cut it for a family of three and a pregnant wife. I had two friends in the building business, and they agreed to help me add on, and did most of the work. I did some too, to keep the costs down.

My cousin had an old Datsun 1600 convertible sports car that he kept in my grandmother's garage. We thought the block was cracked, but a few of my friends did not think so. I bought the car for a couple hundred bucks and later found out that the block was not cracked, but a lot of engine work had to be done. I am not a mechanic, but I took off the head and took it to a machine shop. They did a bunch of things and I put it back on, and tried to adjust everything. My neighbor, who is a jack of all trades, got the car running. He later painted it for a motorcycle helmet. I bought a new top and painfully installed it like I knew what I was doing. After it was running, I took my seven month pregnant wife camping. That was not real smart on my part, but we still had a good time, and it was cheap. We sold the other car and could now afford the two we had.

Doing things usually takes me more time. If my wife were to help all of the time, time would be saved, but she would also get burnt out. So, sometimes I ask for help, and sometimes I do not. I could probably do more things myself, but I am such a time conscience guy that it does not make sense to me. Why do something in 1 min. that another person could do in 5 seconds? This is something I probably need to evaluate, since I seem to have more time than others. I have gotten better at doing things myself, but more improvement is needed. I do not want to drive my wife crazy doing things for me, but I do need her help sometimes. I think that I am afraid that if I get to independent, my wife will do a lot more things without me. I want her to know that she is more than just a caregiver to me and that I want the best for her. I want her to stick around, too.

It is quite hard to go out and buy things. I can buy things on Amazon, since they already have our credit card number. This makes it easier to buy things, so I have to be careful not to get carried away. A friend of my wife's has volunteered to be my own personal shopper. Whenever an important date comes up, she helps me buy things for my wife. This has worked out great. My wife can still get a present and not always know what it is. Every now and then I get something that requires installation. I cannot always do it, so I have to rely on someone else to do it. If it is in my son's area of expertise, he can do it. If not, there is nothing like a little gift card to help get things done. It is not expected, but I think it sends a message that it is really appreciated and the person will be more likely to come back and help again.

I cannot drive, so I have to depend on my wife to go somewhere. There are always errands to run, and my wife does them all. I would like to help, but that is not possible. Many times, we will tack an errand on after we have gone somewhere. I will wait in the car and listen to the radio while my wife does something. If it is longer than 30 min., I start to get antsy, so we try not to take too much time doing these things. We have got it down very well and usually get things done right the first time. If we have to go back to a place, it is a drag.

The circulation in my legs could be a lot better. My feet get very cold during the winter months, so my wife bought me an electric lap blanket one Christmas. It works well. I used to get into bed with really cold feet and my wife would let me know about it. Summertime is no problem, but winters can be bad. We have an electric fire place, but it sucks up too much electricity and our heating bill was very high. We do not use it now that I have the electric blanket, but my wife says it is cold in certain areas of the house. We turned up the heat a little, but my wife is still cold. I do not notice it, because of the blanket, but I believe her. I will have to ask the doctor next time about circulation problems.

My "sense of urgency" gets me frustrated. If I ask something, I usually think that people will get back to me soon. That is not always the case. If someone says to me, "Let me think about it", or "I'll get back to you on that", and then never gets back to me, I do not appreciate that. People are busy, and it is easy to forget, but I think it is not always good. I need to remember that forgetting something is not the end of the world. It will happen and I need to realize that. Sometimes, I ask my wife for something and there is no hurry. I usually get it sooner than I expect, as my wife does not want to forget. That is fine with me. I am not so busy, and do not have as much to remember. I see my wife text questions or ask things on the phone, and not get answered. People are busy, but a quick answer is better than no answer. Many times, my wife has to text or call again. This all takes more time, and that is something that is precious.

I am not alone, as everyone has frustrations. Mine happen to deal with independence, primarily. Other people have their own frustrations, and deal with them. Since I usually do not like asking others to do things for me, I have to learn to deal with these situations. God can grant me the peace, but it can be so hard to wait.

❦{ 11 }❦

HOPE

So, what does the future hold for me? I want to be treated as reasonably normal. My wife, boys, and others know I need some help, and I do not want them to think of me as just a selfish person. I call it self-preservation, but others would think I'm just thinking of myself. I hope they will understand this. Fortunately, they cannot walk in my shoes and know what it is like. I want to see my boys succeed and give where we can. Giving too much, however, is not necessarily helping. One can start to feel entitled and I do not want that. I spend a lot of time reading and doing things on the computer. Unfortunately, most people see me in front of the TV. This is not always a good image, but I am not sure what to do about it.

I tend to be a "glass is half full" kind of person. Sometimes, I probably have too much trust in others. Fortunately, we have enough and can make a few mistakes. I am not saying that this is good, but it is easier to make decisions if money is not a major issue. We are to use our money wisely, at least, that is what I think God wants. It would be easy to think that if one trusts God, it is okay to use all one' s money. However, there are responsibilities to one's family, and that is biblically important. Trusting in God is like a two edged sword. If one trusts completely, but does not take care of family, that is not right. Since we are all sinners, I suspect this is where this comes into play. One can think they have great intent, but deep down, something else may be happening that we are not aware of. This is theology at its finest, what to do? Everyone has their own worldview, whether they know it or not. The Christian world view centers on faith and trust. However, most other religions allow the person to be in charge, and that is very dangerous and relative. There is no longer room for absolutes. I think it is sad when we always have to be in charge.

I tend to laugh a lot. Hopefully, that is taken as a positive sign and not a negative one. There is another great song by

Dan Hicks, called The Laughing Song. This funny song has some guy laughing so much that his uncle has him put away in a mental institution. I do not laugh that much, but I believe that laughter is much better than negativity. I think it is healthier, too. It is too easy to feel bad about something, when you do not need to. Most of the time, I would rather assume that God knows what is happening, and it is okay, even if I do not like it.

I cannot continue to do the same thing day after day. I need to have some goals. I would like to see my in-laws, and brother-in-law and his family, have some financial stability. Since the men are both ministers, there is not a lot of money floating around. I am not rich, but I could help them with some good financial planning. Our house is in good financial order, so I think I would be heard. I bought 10 Apple shares for my youngest son at $35 apiece. Now they are worth over $500 apiece. However, I also bought my oldest son some Sun shares, but they were bought by Oracle. That was not too good.

I can invest small amounts of money in the stock market. So far, I have done okay, but it could be better. I ask a broker friend for advice, but I do not like to do a whole lot of research on the various companies. One could investigate all kinds of areas, but I just do not have the will to do it. I am more of a "investigate a little, feel a lot" person, and that is not always smart. I like to think that if I made a lot of money I could give it away. However, we had some friends who bought an ice cream shop and any profits would go to Christian causes. Unfortunately, some staff took advantage of the situation. The business folded, and the friends' dreams were not realized. They moved on and are doing fine, but God chose to work in their lives a little differently than they had expected. If I can make more money, I will give most of it away. However, making money is not my goal. We will see what happens.

I am not sure what is in store for me, but I do know that I do not want to give up on life. I want my family to have a normal life, but I am not sure what that is supposed to look like. The Man upstairs has given me a wild road to be on, with many challenges, and I hope He will be pleased with how they have been handled. I have made plenty of mistakes, but through it all I still believe that God loves me, and wants His best for me. His best is not always the same as mine, so I have to trust.

My wife and I are currently volunteer co-chairs of the local Young Life Committee. Since I have some leadership experience from the past, and my wife went to the Young Life club as a high school student, we have a clue what we are dealing with. Unfortunately, money is always a big factor. Getting people to help with fund raising is a challenge, but the staff people are great in helping. There always seems to be a challenge and we like to think that we are helping. We have a committee of approximately 11 people. They are all great people and help where they can. We all know that God is in control. We just need to try and figure out where he is taking us. I believe we are doing some good, and kids are meeting God where they are living.

I have a verse that I cling to in James, Chapter 1, verses 2 through 5. My sanity has been questioned for holding onto this thought: "Consider it all joy, my brethren, when you encounter various trials, knowing that the testing of your faith produces endurance. And let endurance have its perfect result, that you may be complete, lacking in nothing." What does joy have to do with this waiting room I have been put in? Joy is not a happy feel good emotion. It is the depth of my soul that holds peace and hope in Someone greater than me, who has my best interests at heart. I have faith in this.

Glossary

Amoxicillin: A medication under the same
                    category as penicillin usually used
                    in respiratory and ear infections.

Augmentin: A type of penicillin used for ear
                    infections as well as respiratory.

Babesia: A malaria like parasitic disease
                    caused by Babesia in ticks.

Bechet's: A rare disorder, chronic
                    inflammation in blood vessels,
                    possibly an auto-immune
                    disorder.

CAT: Computerized Axial Tomography.
                    An x-ray procedure of "sections"
                    of the body.

CBC:	Complete blood count, red blood cells and differentiated white cells.
Cerebellum:	"Lower Brain" region of the brain that has a role in motor control.
Cerebral Angiogram:	A diagnostic procedure providing images of the blood vessels in the brain or head.
Cytoxan:	A drug used for Chemo therapy in breast or Ovarian cancer and Hodgkins Lymphoma and Leukemias, causing cell death. Epstein Barr or EBV: A virus causing mononucleosis
EEG:	Electroencephleograph, study of brain waves.
ELISA test:	An analytic biochemistry assay diagnostic tool to analyze antigen quantities.
Gamma Globulin:	Immune serum for primary immunodeficiency which increases ones antibody titers.
GPS:	Global positioning satellite, device used for directions.

Herx-heimer: A reaction often given after a treatment given for Lyme disease, characterized by fever, diarrhea, nausea and sweats.

Homeopathic: Herbal related medicines to regulate health.

Imuran: A medication that suppresses the immune system. When used with steroids fewer steroids are required. iPod: A small device for listening to music.

Labrynthitis: Inflammation of the inner ear causing imbalance.

L'bri Fellowship: Christian Conference ground founded by Francis Schaeffer.

Lumbar Puncture: A diagnostic test to tap cerebral spinal fluid with a long needle from the lumbar area.

Lupus: A chronic inflammatory multisystem disease of the immune system. An autoimmune disease.

Lyme disease:	The most common tick borne disease in North America and Europe. Caused by Borrelia Burgdorferi, usually in deer ticks.
Lymphatoid Granulomatosis:	A rare Epstein Barr viral disease characterized by B-cell Lymphoma.
Lymphoma:	A cancer of the immune system.
MRI:	Magnetic Resonance Imaging. Without using ionizing radiation.
Neurologist:	A physician who specialties in neurology trained to investigate neurological disorders.
Neurosarcodosis:	A condition featuring granulomas various tissues involving brain and spinal cord.
Nystagmus:	Involuntary eye movement caused by central nervous system disorders.
Paxil:	A medication used as an antidepressant.

Penicillin: A medication used to kill bacteria. Most effective against fast growing bacteria.

PET scan: Positron emission tomography. Locates increase in metabolic activity in the body to locate cancers.

Phenergan: A medication used in nausea and vomiting to suppress the condition.

Plantanos: Banana like fruit.

Plasmaphoresis: A process using dialysis equipment takes ones blood and is treated with cell solution, then returned to the body with harmful antibodies removed.

Pons: A structure located on the brain stem that relays signals dealing with swallow, sleep, breathing and equilibrium.

Prednisone: A medication to suppress immunity by reducing inflammation by disrupting processes in white blood cells.

Prozac:	A medication that inhibits serotonin reuptake and treats mood Problems, such as depression.
Pulmonary embolism:	A blockage of an artery in the lungs caused by air or blood clot or tumor cells.
Rheumatologist:	A clinician that deals with problems of joints, soft tissues and autoimmune diseases & vasculitis.
Rituximab:	A monoclonal antibody given intravenously.
Rocephin:	An anti-infective given in septicemia a bacteria killer.
Sarcoid:	Inflammatory cells in different areas of the body resulting from abnormal immune response.
Solumedrol:	A strong anti-inflammatory drug often given intravenously.
Steriotactic brain biopsy:	A minimally invasive surgery to biopsy a lesion in the brain, burr holes need to be drilled.

Steroid:

A substance that comes from plants or animals that regulates metabolism and immune function.

Strabismus:

Vision problem that is manifested by cross-eyed.

Tegretol:

A drug used for complex partial seizures or mixed seizure patterns.

Tournament boat:

Inboard water ski boat with platform in the back and smaller wake.

Western Blot test:

A test for Lyme more sensitive in screening Borreliosis.

Whipples:

A rare systemic infection caused by bacterium Trophergma Whipple, commonly considered a gastrointestinal disorder.

Zithromax:

A medication that kills bacteria based infections usually respiratory/sinus infection, caused by influenza or staph and streptococcus aureus.

CPSIA information can be obtained at www.ICGtesting.com
Printed in the USA
BVOW041833301112

306949BV00001B/5/P